ALSO BY TED KERASOTE

Bloodties

Navigations

Heart of Home

HEART
of
HOME

People, Wildlife, Place

Ted Kerasote

VILLARD NEW YORK

Some of the essays in this work have appeared in *Bugle, Gray's Sporting Journal,
Jackson Hole, Orion,* and *Sports Afield.* In addition, "A Talk About Ethics" was
originally published as "To Preserve the Hunt" in *Orion,* and as "Restoring the
Older Knowledge" in *A Hunter's Heart,* edited by David Petersen; "The Back
Bend" was originally published as "Solitaire" in *Sports Afield* and in *Home Waters,*
edited by Gary Soucie; "Logging" was originally published in *The Nature of
Nature,* edited by William Shore.

Library of Congress Cataloging-in-Publication Data
Kerasote, Ted.
Heart of home : people, wildlife, place / Ted Kerasote.
p.   cm.
ISBN 0-679-45012-2 (alk. paper)
I. Hunting—Anecdotes.   2. Fishing—Anecdotes.   3. Kerasote,
Ted—Journeys   4. Hunting—Philosophy.   5. Fishing—Philosophy.
I. Title
SK33.K44   1998
814'.54—dc21   97-17913

Random House website address: http://www.randomhouse.com/

Printed in the United States of America on acid-free paper

24689753

First Edition

Book design and illustration by Lilly Langotsky

for G. K.

Acknowledgments

Thanks to Kim Fadiman for his reading and commentary; to Allison von Maur for her reading, commentary, and loving support; and to Scott, April, and Tessa Landale, my Ditch Creek family.

Contents

Prologue

Ever since Izaak Walton published *The Compleat Angler, or the Contemplative Man's Recreation* in 1653, fishing, or at least fly-fishing for trout, has been seen as a gentle pursuit, a balm for the harried soul, a retreat from the worlds of commerce and politics.

No doubt this is why CEOs the world over have adopted it, and companies like Orvis have made the selling of flies and elegant rods to well-heeled men and women into a multimillion-dollar business. When the going gets rough, you can take Prozac or buy a fly rod.

But who said it better than Walton himself? Anglers, wrote the ironmonger turned fishing writer, "enjoy what the other possess and enjoy not, for Anglers, and meek, quiet-spirited men, are free from those high, those restless thoughts, which corrode the sweets of life; and they, and they only, can say, as the Poet has happily expressed it:—

> *"Hail! blest estate of lowliness!*
> *Happy enjoyments of such minds,*

As, rich in self-contentedness,
Can, like the reeds in roughest winds,
   By yielding make that blow but small
   At which proud oaks and cedars fall."

The Chinese poet Lao-tzu wrote more eloquently about "going with the flow," but Walton sold more copies. In fact, no book other than the Bible and the Book of Common Prayer has been more often reprinted.

Hunting has not fared as well, even back in the times before "animal rights" became a household term. Montaigne, writing in 1578, fifteen years before the father of angling was born, said, "For myself, I have not even been able without distress to see pursued and killed an innocent animal which is defenseless and which does us no harm." Trout, even by such sensitive souls as Montaigne, were not cut such slack.

In the four hundred years since Walton and Montaigne wrote, perceptions of fishing and hunting haven't changed all that much. Indeed, the authors of a 1994 study called *Attitudes of the Uncommitted Public Toward Wildlife Management* might just as well have gone directly to Walton and Montaigne and saved the wildlife agencies their money.

When the pollsters asked "the uncommitted public" in St. Louis, Atlanta, Phoenix, and Cherry Hill, New Jersey, to compare fishing and hunting, they found that fishing was thought more benign, serene, and family-oriented; that fishing included more women and the elderly; and that it was considered less violent.

"Fish in a bucket," said the public, "were less upsetting than a deer in the back of a pickup." In addition, fish were seen as lower species than mammals or birds, and fish made the decision to be caught, plus you could release them. They were cold-blooded, everyone agreed, and therefore easier to kill than warm-blooded animals and birds. As one person from New Jersey put it, "You can't look a fish in the eyes."

Opinions about anglers and hunters themselves were just as one-sided. Anglers were seen as "caring, artistic, and patient." They were "kind" individuals, immersed in family values, not half as macho as hunters, and they were "philosophers." Hunters, almost universally, were seen as "beer-drinking, redneck" people who "wore camouflage to work for a week."

This is not earthshaking news. It only puts words to the numbers. In the United States and Canada about 17 million people hunt. Thirty-six million people fish (this doesn't include children, who don't have to buy a license, and whose participation raises the fishing population to between 40 and 60 million individuals, depending on whose numbers you want to believe). Worldwide, the pattern is similar, with greater participation in and approval of fishing and smaller participation in and disapproval of or uneasiness about hunting.

When you consider that few of us go about the messy business of catching or growing our daily food, such attitudes about fishing and hunting aren't all that surprising. Removed from strong and original sentiments, we shrink at the sight of blood. Yet if the popularity of nature documentaries and adventure travel are any testament, we still long for a taste of our primal condition. It should be little wonder that the rise in popularity of catch-and-release fishing matches the rise in consumption of decaffeinated coffee in developed nations. In the case of fishing, you get the smell, the taste, and a bit of the buzz of the real thing—being a predator and touching the mystery of life's departure—without all the unpleasant side effects: a bloody carcass and an actual death on your hands.

The essays in this book come in both decaf and regular varieties, and reflect the communal sentiment about fishing and hunting. I have had some very funny times fishing and have enjoyed writing about them in a lighthearted way. All my hunting stories turn out more serious. Maybe this is because we tolerate, even love, a jokester and bumbler with fly rod in hand. Often we have been that very person, snapping off flies, falling in the river, hopelessly clumsy but having a wonderful time. Comedians with guns, we lock up.

When these essays do turn serious, whether they're about fishing or hunting, they often deal with the same subject treated by the first storytellers of fishing and hunting, the shamans throwing fat on the fire, and the cave painters in their dark tunnels, propitiating the souls of animals with ocher: Which of the deaths that we cause are okay and which are not?

Until recently hunter-gatherer societies enforced the okay/not okay rule with taboos, like not mixing the blood of land and sea animals, not sleeping with your spouse before you went off hunting, and apologizing to the animal you were about to kill, literally asking for its life to feed your family. And though the rules of the hunter-gatherers were strict, they were evenhanded, not discriminating against any one group of hunters.

By contrast, monarchical societies, particularly in Europe, evolved codes of sportsmanship to guide the nobility's behavior toward wildlife. In the process, the common hunter was disenfranchised. A king or queen—killing a stag to the accompaniment of hounds and heralds, and nicely putting a farewell sprig of evergreen in its mouth—became the hero of a minstrel's song. If caught killing the same deer, even to feed his family, a commoner had his ears cut off, or could be executed. Robin Hood was the most famous of these poacher-heroes who waged war against what was correctly perceived as grand larceny: Wildlife, once held in common, had become the property of the few. Today, in Europe, huntable wildlife remains the property of the wealthy.

The United States, with its values of self-sufficiency and democracy, institutionalized what Robin Hood fought for. Mixing European sporting customs with frontier and hunter-gatherer traditions, it made wildlife "owned" by the people, capable of being slain by anyone of age and under certain well-defined circumstances, which often included a degree of seasonal pageantry, the fall hunt. Canada, even though part of the Commonwealth, followed suit, creating a continent-wide body of wildlife laws that, far removed from shamanistic times, still tries to answer the nagging question of the women and men who sifted bones through campfires: How do we kill animals and make their deaths okay? We may use a computer model instead of ashes to predict when and which species we may hunt, but some of the intent is the same: elk and geese may be rightfully killed only in season; bald eagles can no longer be killed at all. The species, the date, even a few yards (inside or outside a national park), make a difference.

When it comes to telling the stories of fishing and hunting in North America, the continent's writers, by and large, have followed the halcyon tradition of Walton, praising the peace to be found in nature and the healthful merits of a life lived in the outdoors. Only occasionally have writers turned to the older shamanistic tradition of discussing those deaths that can be allowed and those that cannot. Politics, however, has finally caught up with outdoor literature, forcing more and more of us who ply the trade of nature writing to turn to the uncomfortable issues of equity and fairness, and of what happens to sport when one decides to go beyond codes of sportsmanship.

The following essays begin with Walton's tradition and quickly find the path of disquieting questions and slippery answers. Is "playing" cold-blooded fish ("tormenting" is the term used by animal rightists) and calling it "sport" something that we want to do if fish really feel pain? Is the old way of catching, killing, and eating fish the more moral thing to do? How about killing warm-blooded deer, barbecuing their steaks, and putting their antlers over our hearths? In the age of the supermarket, is this legitimate subsistence hunting and an appropriate form of honor . . . or barbarism? Can urban people, who see wildlife infrequently, participate in such activities?

Those of us who need clear-cut, legally enforced responses to some of these issues—as do the far left of the animal welfare movement, which wants to eradicate all fishing and hunting, and the far right of the hunting community, which wants to circle the wagons and defend all of it—may not find much value in the questions these stories pose, full as they are of paradox and ambiguity, and the annoying trait of otherwise reasonable individuals to swerve in their habits: to be vegetarians who wear leather boots, to be committed hunters who will kill an elk but who won't shoot a bear, to be anglers who will play a trout to within an inch of its life but who condemn their neighbor for the deer she kills with one shot.

About such inconsistencies, I have no better advice than that given by the poet Rainer Maria Rilke. "Love *the questions themselves*," he said. "Perhaps then, someday far in the future, you will gradually, without even noticing it, live your way into the answer."

In living out the questions generated by fishing and hunting—living them out attentively, constantly, and with care and compassion—one also discovers an unforseen reward: escape. Just as

Izaak Walton found angling a refuge from the civil war of his era, those of us who participate in the cycles of nature through fishing, hunting, or just walking through the outdoors, can find succor from the serial wars and environmental degradation of ours. Not that any of us should think that if we leave for some pristine river or mountain range that our problems will go away. Instead, after we have done what we can do in our home places— gone to the public meetings and to the ballot box, written letters to our political representatives, and contributed to organizations that preserve habitat and lobby for wildlife—we still need to *participate*, to plunge our hands into the consonant and sometimes poignant beauty, the authentic living and dying, that remain on the planet.

It's not a perfect world, but it does have its moments of sublime music. These are the lyrics I've put to the songs, and a few of the questions I continue to ask.

Heart of Home

FATHERS

When I was a teenager, in the 1960s, the world was a darker place. Sunlight wasn't the issue; the issue was the speed at which people and information traveled. The Interstate Highway System had only recently been started, we still went to Europe by ship, and a letter from my Venezuelan pen pal took a month to arrive. When information came, it came in black and white, the first grainy film clips from Vietnam sometimes days or weeks old, the men who had fallen in firefights already cold and in the ground. As for CNN, faxes, and the Internet, they were barely a dream.

I was also spending a lot of time in the actual dark, trying to know better the fish and birds who moved around my Long Island home under starlight and in the foggy dusks as easily as my cousin Pete and I moved around during the day.

He was my brother in rod and arms (we were born only six months apart), and together we fished for striped bass, meeting the tides at 2, 3, 4 A.M., catching enormous alabaster fish with sea-green stripes with no witnesses except ourselves, the surf, and the wind. Around the winter solstice, he and I would sit for entire days in our small boat, surrounded by a chicken-wire stockade of cattails and rushes, as Oyster Bay turned to slush and the flocks of scaup, scraggly charcoal lines on the horizon, broke and wheeled, attracted to our decoys. Sometimes there were also Canada geese, their honking in the somnolent twilight a lonesome and lovely message from the tundra, those empty and dreamlike places of my imaginings that the great birds made palpable as I held their gray-and-white bodies in my hands.

As for our fathers, they gave us enthusiastic support and equipment, to be sure, but not direction. Pete's father liked baseball and mine cycling, and when Pete and I became incoherently excited about a run of bluefish or a flight of mallards, they seemed uncomfortable, as if they were unsure about whose seed might have sired these pagans. In some ways, their being fans and not participants was to the good—Pete and I made it up as we went along. Many times it was all so damn perplexing. When it was ten minutes after legal shooting hour, and the birds were pouring into our decoys, Pete and I turned to each other, not to our fathers, and tried to decide between the law and lust. When we saw men release a bony and barely edible bergal but purposefully slam it against the side of the boat, killing it, there was no one to talk to about what, even to boys, seemed wasteful and heartless.

Now when I visit Oyster Bay and see its shores covered with houses, it is hard to believe that Pete and I walked along its waters on dirt roads and through head-high grass, our shotguns over our shoulders like country boys out of *Huckleberry Finn.* The post–World War II explosion of suburbia had only just begun, and we still lived a rural life within forty miles of New York City, our coves and forested hills empty of both houses and fear. I don't ever remember locking a door, not even against the many ghosts the countryside still held: George Washington, who had slept down the road; Theodore Roosevelt, TR, whose estate stood just across the bay; and nameless Indian boys who, like ourselves, had speared the shad who ran up Mill Creek. Back then, in our wonderful naïveté, we still called them "Indians" because we, the grandchildren of immigrants, thought of ourselves as "native Americans."

Sometimes, in the lazy last days of summer, when the fish weren't biting, I rode my bike along the cove road, through the sleepy town of Oyster Bay and up to Sagamore Hill, where Roosevelt had lived. Theodores abounded in our family, and my mother kept the tradition going by naming me after my paternal grandfather. For me, though, the coincidence of having the same name as the Rough Rider and African hunter was far more pleasing.

Out of some subconscious magician's hat, my mother had plucked John for my middle name, a move that made the family question her sanity, since there wasn't a John to be found in the clan. I, on the other hand, thought that she had exhibited good taste, naming me after my other hero, John Muir, who did what Roosevelt could not: explore for the sake of exploring, bringing home neither life list nor trophy, counting a dance in a thunderstorm a good day's work.

It was a treat, after the long bike ride to Sagamore Hill, to sit in the deep leather armchairs of TR's library, under the doleful eyes of the Cape buffalo TR had brought home from Kenya, and read of his adventures and of the adventures of Muir, whose books I had also read. If someone had asked me, at the age of sixteen, to explain the difference between Roosevelt and Muir in the terms we now use—as the respective fathers of the conservation and preservation movements—I couldn't have. But I knew then, as well as I knew my own two names, that the men I cared for so deeply represented two very different directions of the spirit, two directions that pulled me first one way then another, yet which I knew to have been born from the same womb: the love of country. Both men also had the endearing trait of opining on the subject about which the sports magazines I read were consistently silent: how much power one could exert over the world without becoming evil.

When I pieced together, one afternoon there in the library, that Roosevelt and Muir had been more than correspondents, that they had actually met, ridden into the high country of Yosemite together, and camped, I was ecstatic. I felt as if my spiritual ancestors must have had the conversation that had taken place so many times within myself, as I knocked striped bass over the head or, feeling sorry for their struggle, released them . . . as the birds flew into our decoys with enough light to shoot but after the legal clock had run out.

The year was 1903, and TR, wearing a broad-brimmed western hat and with a bandanna knotted around his throat, climbed aboard the stage coach to Wawona, California. At forty-five, he had already been president for nearly two years, and he still retained his powerful physique despite the stomach he had put on since the Spanish-American War. Then, at the head of the Rough Riders, he had charged up Kettle Hill, bullets whining around him. Drawing his revolver, he bowled over a Spanish trooper "neatly as a jackrabbit." Now, in California, eyes flashing behind his pince-nez, teeth leering from his enormous chimp's grin, he raised his hands to the onlookers, ducked inside the stage, and began to listen to Muir, whom he admired for his nature writing and his campaigns to save America's vanishing forests. In fact, before this political swing through the West, he had written to Muir, asking him to be his guide in Yosemite. "I do not want anyone with me but you," he wrote, "and I want to drop politics absolutely for four days and just be out in the open with you."

Gray-bearded, hollow-cheeked, ascetic, and looking ridiculous in the new yellow suit he had bought for the occasion, Muir directed the president to a window and sat behind him. The long-awaited moment to turn the president's ear had arrived.

"There are the first big trees, Mr. President."

"Mr. Muir." TR turned to his guide. "It is good to be with you."

Reaching Yosemite's south entrance and disembarking, Roosevelt asked for his valise, which was nowhere to be seen. The Yosemite Park Commission—intent on keeping the valley under state jurisdiction and knowing that Muir would present a case for federal control—had sent the president's luggage ahead to a banquet they had scheduled.

"*Get it!*" snapped TR.

Muir thought that he had never heard two words spoken so much like bullets.

The two men didn't wait for the bag to arrive. They mounted horses and rode off into the great trees, making camp in a grove that TR called a "more beautiful cathedral than was ever conceived by any human architect." In the stillness of the evening, the flames of the campfire crackling, a hermit thrush sang, and it astonished the president that John Muir, the naturalist, geologist, and mountaineer, couldn't identify the bird. Muir, on the other hand, was surprised that the cowboy, war hero, and politician "knew so much natural history."

Like many famous men, each lived within the walls of his specialty—Roosevelt was one of the leading ornithologists and mammalogists of his day, while Muir was an amazingly keen observer of natural processes, especially geology, and an ecologist who saw the whole while ignoring some of the specifics.

The next day, while their aides, hangers-on, and commissioners took stages into the valley, TR and Muir ascended on horseback through forest and snow patches to Glacier Point. As the sun set, they camped without tents on the point's summit, cooking steaks over an open fire. After dinner, TR leaned back against his saddle, stretched his feet to the fire, laced his fingers around his mug of coffee, and declared, "Now, *this* is bully!"

Muir, making up their beds of fern and cedar boughs, looked up with a mischievous grin and said, "Watch this." Taking some flaming brands from the campfire, he ignited a dead pine tree that stood alone on a rocky point. As the flames soared up the dry branches, he began dancing a jig around it. Roosevelt, catching the older man's enthusiasm, leapt up before the enormous torch. Hopping from one foot to the other, he shouted, "Hurrah! Hurrah! That's a candle it took five hundred years to make. Hurrah for Yosemite, Mr. Muir!"

It was an innocent age, an age in which both men had had the good fortune to walk through the first bloom of what history would think of as a change in consciousness.

Muir began his journey of self-exploration by walking from Kentucky to the Gulf of Mexico—a thousand miles through the Reconstruction South. He carried no more than a plant press and a bag containing his toilet articles, a change of underwear, and three books: the New Testament; the poems of Robbie Burns; and *Paradise Lost.* He took no blankets, no tent, and no weapon, and he chose the "wildest, leafiest, and least trodden way" he could find, even though the country he crossed was full of marauding bandits left over from the Civil War. He assumed that he would be thought an impoverished herb doctor and would be left alone. The bluff worked, or perhaps a pure and invincible glow had begun to shine about him. On the inside cover of his journal he had written, "John Muir, Earth-planet, Universe." In its pages he began to describe the physical landscape he crossed—"Many rapid streams, flowing in beautiful flower-bordered cañons embosomed in dense woods"—as well as the spiritual one that was forming within him: "Let children walk with Nature, let them see the beautiful blendings and communions of death and life, their joyous inseparable unity, as taught in woods and meadows, plains and mountains and streams of our blessed star, and they will learn that death is stingless indeed, and as beautiful as life, and that the grave has no victory, for it never fights. All is divine harmony." For John Muir, Earth-planet, Universe, even rocks were endowed "with a sensation of a kind that we in our blind exclusive perfection can have no manner of communication with." What we now call deep ecology and holistic resource management, as well as bits and pieces of New Age environmental philosophy, were born on this walk.

Muir reached the Gulf of Mexico, set off for California by ship, and, arriving on its shore, walked inland to the Sierra Nevada, his "Range of Light." There, he chipped at the rocks with a geologist's pick, counted the petals of flowers, and listened to birdsong (though he didn't always bother to find out the name of the species whose song he was enjoying). He climbed mountains where no other person had set foot and left no name on their summits to commemorate his first ascents. Staring across the ranges of jagged summits, he predicted glaciers where no one believed them to be, then hiked into the wilderness and found the moving ice. Unarmed, he walked to within a dozen yards of grizzlies; he sang to squirrels; he stood on the edge of Yosemite Falls, imagining himself a drop of water cascading in rainbows to the valley below. "You bathe in these spirit-beams," he exulted, "turning round and round, as if warming at a camp-fire. Presently you lose consciousness of your own separate existence: you blend with the landscape, and become part and parcel of nature."

Sometimes, though, becoming part and parcel of nature created turmoil for Muir. One day, after climbing Mount Shasta, he descended to find four big-game hunters at his camp. Three, to his delight, were from his homeland, Scotland; one was from England. They had been fishing and deer hunting for several weeks and now wanted to kill a wild sheep, "not only for the sport of the thing," Muir wrote, "but to learn their habits and to see their wild homes, and get specimens with which to adorn their halls."

At this point in his life, Muir had spent five years in Yosemite, observing wildlife, keeping careful field notes, and, unlike other naturalists of his day, forgoing any collecting that involved rifle or shotgun. As a boy, he had hunted birds and small mammals for the pot on his family's homestead in Wisconsin, but he did it with mixed feelings, often regretting the deaths he had caused. As he said about passenger pigeons: "Oh, what bonnie, bonnie birds! . . . It's awfu' like a sin to kill them!" Only twice as an adult had he killed wildlife. Even though in both cases they had been rattlesnakes, and he had believed himself threatened, he had felt "degraded by the killing business, farther from heaven." Nonetheless, he decided to accompany the hunters, hoping to see the animals whom he considered the finest of the Sierra's mountaineers.

After several days on the mountain, the party discovered a herd of fifty bighorns, and the hunters shot and wounded a ram and ewe. The rest of the herd continued over the crest of a ridge, and the hunters reloaded. As they approached the wounded ram, he rose and fled, not pausing until he reached the skyline. There he stopped, giving his pursuers a last glimpse of his "noble horns." Catching his breath, Muir felt astonished at his emotions.

"We little know how much wildness there is in us," he wrote. "Only a few generations separate us from our grandfathers that were savage as wolves. This is the secret of our love for the hunt. Savageness is natural, civilization is strained and unnatural. . . . In the excitement and savage exhilaration of the pursuit of the wounded, I, who have never killed any mountain life, felt like a wolf chasing the flying flock. But all this ferocity soon passed away, and we were Christians again."

A little farther on, the party discovered the wounded ewe. "She was breathing still, but helpless, and I pitied her," Muir said. "A moment before, unarmed as I was, I could have worried her like a wolf, but helpless, and with so gentle an eye, she inspired pity as if she were human."

They killed her for the pot, ate her that evening, and though Muir was ambiguous as to whether he partook of the meal, it would not be surprising if he had. Preferring bread and tea as his wilderness ration, he wasn't averse to eating everything from gull eggs to fried porpoise on his adventures, saying of humanity's predatory place among other species, "Plants, animals, and stars are all kept in place, bridled along appointed ways, *with* one another, and *through the midst* of one another—killing and being killed, eating and being eaten, in harmonious proportions and quantities. . . . Wild lambs eat as many wild flowers as they can find or desire, and men and wolves eat the lambs to just the same extent."

In his early forties, having published many essays about the need to preserve parks and forests, Muir came down from the mountains. He married the daughter of a wealthy fruit rancher and took charge of his father-in-law's business. Abandoning the wilderness for nine months of the year to tend his orchards, he became a financial success, and his writings from that period reflect his utilitarian concerns: "I suppose we need not go mourning the buffaloes. In the nature of things they had to give place to better cattle, though the change might have been made without barbarous wickedness. Likewise many of nature's five hundred kinds of wild trees had to make way for orchards and cornfields."

The cost of such a utilitarian bargain was high, and no one knew it better than Muir himself. Wracked by a bronchial cough, made worse by the dusty climate of his California ranch, he annually left his wife and daughters for the Sierra or the coast of Alaska. Health and equanimity restored after a few months, he told the nation what he had learned in the wild: "Thousands of tired, nerve-shaken, over-civilized people are beginning to find out that going to the mountains is going home; that wildness is a necessity; and that mountain parks and reservations are useful not only as fountains of timber and irrigating rivers, but as fountains of life." He gave this idea political shape by helping to found the Sierra Club in 1892, and he served as its president until his death in 1914.

Approaching those last years, Muir had a change of heart about how a person might join what as a young man he had called the "completeness of . . . the cosmos." Sounding almost as if he were a born-again Christian or his own Calvinist father, trying to restrain the wayward boy he himself had been, Muir wrote,

> Surely a better time must be drawing nigh when godlike human beings will become truly humane, and learn to put their animal fellow mortals in their hearts instead of on their backs or in their dinners. In the mean time we may just as well as not learn to live clean, innocent lives instead of slimy, bloody ones. All hale, red-blooded boys are savage, the best and boldest the savagest, fond of hunting and fishing. But when thoughtless childhood is past, the best rise the highest above all this bloody flesh and sport business, the wild foundational animal dying out day by day, as divine uplifting, transfiguring charity grows in.

TR, who would receive the brunt of Muir's twilight musings about what the future would call "animal rights," was an even more complex study in incongruities. A delicate, asthmatic child born to wealthy Manhattan parents in 1858, he made himself healthy through calisthenics and by snowshoeing through the Maine woods in pursuit of moose and deer. The tough work of chasing large animals through wild country and rendering them into food and trophies came to represent physical and mental health for TR—what he was fond of calling "the strenuous life."

It was little surprise to his family that lands wilder than upstate New York soon called him. As a young man, he bought a cattle ranch in the Dakota Territory and went from being a smooth New York socialite to a tanned, mustachioed, and husky cowboy in chaps and bandanna, from a dude to a respected cattle boss in less than a year. The respect was honestly won. Confronted by a drunken wrangler who tried to knock off his glasses with shouts of "Four-eyes!" TR rose from his bar stool and coldcocked the bully on the jaw. Another time, alone on the prairie, he found himself being ridden down by five Indians brandishing carbines. He dismounted, leveled his rifle at the braves, and stood them off with nothing more than a steady aim. As he said, "Indians—and for the matter of that, white men—do not like to ride in on a man who is cool and means shooting." Charged by a grizzly, he stood his ground until the last possible instant, simultaneously firing and leaping aside to avoid the bear's raking claws.

A photograph taken shortly after the incident shows Roosevelt in a tasseled buckskin shirt, trousers, and moccasins, a hunting knife thrust through his cartridge belt, a Winchester rifle in his arms, his proud and accomplished pose the summation of what he had begun to advocate in his books on ranch life and hunting: "The chase is among the best of all national pastimes; it cultivates that vigorous manliness for the lack of which in a nation, as in an individual, the possession of no other qualities can possibly atone."

Nearly a century and a half later, it's all too easy to dismiss the man as one of North America's great jingoists, who served his aspirations to high office by romanticizing the chase of both men and beasts. But that would not take into account the other side of TR, the keen observer and lover of nature.

Concerning the pronghorn antelope, he noted what other Euro-American writers had failed to observe, that "unlike all other hollow-horned animals, it sheds its horns annually." He also compared the gait of the white-tailed and black-tailed deer, delineated the life zones of the Dakotas, and took pleasure in songbirds, which he had first admired in the East. "In the spring when the thickets are green, the hermit-thrushes sing sweetly in them; when it is moonlight, the voluble, cheery notes of the thrashers or brown thrushes can be heard all night long." He was chivalrous as well, at least when his ranch was well stocked with meat. Startled by a white-tailed doe springing before his horse, he said that "there was no reason for harming her and she made a pretty picture as she bound lightly off among the rose-red flowers."

Indeed, in an age that ate everything that walked, crawled, swam, or flew, he went further than mere chivalry. Writing to Frank M. Chapman, an ornithologist at the American Museum of Natural History, TR said, "I would like to see all harmless wild things, but especially all birds, protected in every way. . . . Spring would not be spring without song birds, any more than it would be spring without birds and flowers, and I only wish that besides protecting the songsters, the birds of the grove, the orchard, the garden and the meadow, we could also protect the birds of the seashore and of the wilderness." He went on to suggest how the loon, under wise legislation, could be a feature in every Adirondack lake, how the tanager and cardinal made points of "glowing beauty in the green wood," and how when the bluebirds "were so nearly destroyed by the severe winter a few seasons ago, the loss was like the loss of an old friend, or at least like the burning down of a familiar and dearly loved house." Then, echoing sentiments he had penned as a young boy on tour with his parents in the Middle East (where he compared the escarpments of Moab to a temple), he stated what would eventually become one of the underpinnings of the environmental movement: "The destruction of the Wild Pigeon and the Carolina Paroquet has meant a loss as severe as if the Catskills and the Palisades were taken away. When I hear of the destruction of a species I feel as if all the works of some great writer had perished." If such sentiments weren't enough to set him apart from a time in which stuffed birds decorated women's hats, he also wrote that "wild flowers should be enjoyed unplucked where they grow."

Yet he continued to hunt with a ravenous appetite. On another monthlong trip in the Dakotas, he killed for food and trophies 33 grouse, 21 sage hens, 7 ducks, 2 doves, 11 rabbits, 50 trout, 7 deer, 6 elk, and 3 grizzlies. Ironically, he would one day revile "swinish game-butchers . . . who murder the gravid doe and the spotted fawn with as little hesitation as they would kill a buck of ten points."

His conversion from game slayer to conservationist was prompted by the land itself. On a later visit to the Dakotas, he found the trails lined with buffalo skulls; the skies, once black with pigeons and ducks, were empty. In the breaks, where he had hunted deer and antelope, he saw only dust. A haunting silence lay upon the overgrazed land.

Returning to New York City in 1887, he called together a dinner party of wealthy eastern sportsmen. The club they created, named after two of Roosevelt's heroes, Daniel Boone and Davy Crockett, had two goals: to "promote manly sport with the rifle" and to "work for the preservation of the large game of this country." Only men who had killed three species of American large game with a rifle would be admitted to the Boone and Crockett Club, which restricted its membership to no more than one hundred members, all of whom had the means and influence to advocate the club's agenda at both the state and federal level. Of course, the club's first president was TR.

In the ensuing years the club lobbied for shortened seasons, reduced bag limits, and "fair chase" methods of hunting, such as not shooting game in deep snow or at night. Club members also saw that without habitat there would be no more game. They therefore called for setting aside the nation's forests in protected reserves.

First as governor of New York and then as president, TR lobbied passionately for both goals and was committed to the idea that forests needed to be placed in "inviolable reserves." However, as president he came under the influence of his chief forester, Gifford Pinchot, who had been trained in the sustained-yield theory of European silviculture. Abandoning the concept of forest as inviolable reserve, TR turned toward a more utilitarian concept of conservation. He came to believe that forests must be "conserved" rather than "preserved" and that the utilitarian goal of "the greatest good for the greatest number" meant that the national forests, under scientific management, could be both cut and grazed while simultaneously being "cradles of wildlife."

Together, Pinchot and Roosevelt birthed the ideas of multiple-use public lands and the national forest as tree farm. TR, if one can believe his correspondence and speeches, had few second thoughts about the bargain he had struck—the wilderness pushed back, the deserts reclaimed, the progressive ideas of rationality and perfectibility institutionalized as public policy for the next sixty years, until the Wilderness Act of 1964 idled a few of the chainsaws. TR not only lacked a questioning attitude about the face-lift he was giving North America, he singled out Pinchot, his chief plastic surgeon, for highest praise. "Taking into account the varied nature of the work he did," wrote Roosevelt in his autobiography,

> its vital importance to the nation and the fact that as regards much of it he was practically breaking new ground, and taking into account also his tireless energy and activity, his fearlessness, his complete disinterestedness, his single-minded devotion to the interests of the plain people, and his extraordinary efficiency, I believe it is but just to say that among the many, many public offi-

cials who under my administration rendered literally invaluable service to the people of the United States, he, on the whole, stood first.

Muir, a less purple writer and one less politic, and also one who had a clearer understanding of the effects of clear-cutting and dams, was much shorter about what Pinchot had wrought on the public lands of the United States: "For a parallel to this in downright darkness and idiotic stupidity the records of civilization may be searched in vain."

As Roosevelt had treated forests and rivers, so, too, did he continue to treat wildlife, the fair-chase ethics of the Boone and Crockett Club notwithstanding. "It is always lawful to kill dangerous or noxious animals," he wrote in *The Wilderness Hunter,*

> like the bear, cougar, and wolf; but other game should only be shot when there is need of the meat, or for the sake of an unusually fine trophy. Killing a reasonable number of bulls, bucks, or rams does no harm whatever to the species; to slay half the males of any kind of game would not stop the natural increase, and they yield the best sport, and are the legitimate objects of the chase. Cows, does, and ewes, on the contrary, should only be killed (unless barren) in case of necessity.

It would be unfair, however, to single out TR for holding beliefs that virtually all the great naturalists of his day—John James Audubon, Charles Sheldon, Carl Rungius, and William Hornaday—also held. To a man they were in lockstep with the social Darwinist thinking of the age, ascribing to nature the ethics of the industrial revolution: destruction of strong competitors; sportsmanship for equals; and noblesse oblige toward those who were helpless and weaker. But these hunter-naturalists didn't shape the imaginations and values of future hunters as Roosevelt did. Had he been as visionary as Muir, who perceived animals, even plants and rocks, as possessing spirit and soul, the course of recreational hunting in America might have veered from the competitive and utilitarian course upon which he steered it and to which it has been committed to this day.

When the flames of Muir's five-hundred-year-old torch had died down, he refilled the president's mug with coffee. Pulling a log closer, he said, "There are places where they've left nothing but stumps, Mr. President, where the sheep have grazed the grass to dust. California will do nothing. We need more parks, more forest reserves, federal ones."

He paused, letting Roosevelt look out over the dark landscape, which was quickly clouding over. Finishing his coffee, the president tossed the grounds into the fire and said, "I'll see what I can do, Mr. Muir. For now, I think it smells like snow."

He was right. In the morning, the two men found themselves covered by four inches of powder. Sitting up in his blankets, TR exclaimed, "I told you so. This is bullier yet! I wouldn't miss this for anything."

The sky had cleared, the sun was shining over the eastern divide, and the soaring granite shields glistened brilliantly. Together, Muir and Roosevelt cooked breakfast, Roosevelt continuing to shake his head at the view. Walking to the edge of the summit, he turned, and said, "Mr. Muir, we are not building this country of ours for a day. It has to last through the ages. I'll do my best."

"Thank you, Mr. Roosevelt," said Muir, grinning into the fire.

Deciding to camp one more night together, they rode into the valley, meeting the Yosemite Park Commission, which had planned another banquet.

"There'll be fireworks and searchlights playing upon Yosemite Falls, Mr. President," said the head of the commission, trying to woo him away from Muir's clutches.

"Nature faking, sir," TR said flatly and strode off to speak to the assembled crowd.

"We are not building this country of ours for a day, my friends," he shouted, trying out his new line. "It must last through the centuries." Raising both fists in the air, his typical closing gesture, he descended into the crowd to shake hands. Finally breaking away, he told Muir, "Now, sir, let us see that Bridalveil Meadow of yours."

They mounted and rode toward the last of Muir's promised campgrounds, the old mountaineer pointing out the rock faces that he had scaled in his youth. As night fell, they made a fire, cooked dinner, and brewed a nightcap of strong coffee. The stars came out, the tumble of Bridalveil Falls mixed with the sputtering fire. TR, lying on his saddle blankets, began to reminisce. "Back then, Mr. Muir, around my ranch, there were geese along the rivers, deer in the breaks, and, lord above them all, the bighorn on the rocky heights. I have to agree with you—wonderful essay you wrote, by the way, first-rate observations you had—that wild sheep are the noblest of game. They really test a man's mettle, more than any other hunting."

Muir looked at the fire. Did he dare ruin his chance at federal control of Yosemite over a personal difference—a difference about which, given his experience on Shasta, he couldn't be too holier-than-thou? He took a breath and said, "Mr. Roosevelt, when are you going to get beyond the boyishness of killing things?"

Startled, TR pushed his pince-nez up his nose and looked at the gray scarecrow of a man in the ill-fitting yellow suit.

Staring at the president, Muir pressed home his point. "It seems to me it is all very well for a young fellow who has not formed his standards to rush out in the heat of youth and slaughter animals. I did it myself, but are you not getting far enough along to leave that off?"

Under his mustache, TR chewed his lip.

"Muir," he said uncomfortably, "I guess you are right. You know, once I shot a goshawk out of a tree to avenge missing an eagle on the wing. Bad business. Bad business all around. These days, though, I must tell you, I kill nothing except for meat or scientific purposes. As for you, it's the surroundings of the wilderness that mean the most to me, more than any trophy, more than the game itself." He paused. "Which is why I so value these days with you."

Muir stared at Roosevelt, wishing to believe him. " 'Tis a bonnie world, is it not?"

Roosevelt looked into the darkness. " 'Tis a bonnie world, Mr. Muir," he said softly. "That it is."

A day after leaving the valley, Roosevelt extended the Sierra forest reserve four hundred miles northward to Mount Shasta, and over the next five years he acted upon two of Muir's dreams: He signed the bill that made Yosemite Valley part of the surrounding national park and by executive decree created Grand Canyon National Monument.

Then, his great conservation work done, the forests, he thought, saved from rampant lumbering by Pinchot's scientific management, the Boone and Crockett Club setting standards for hunters, extraordinary landscapes set aside in national parks, and wildlife flourishing in the national refuge system that he had created, he left politics for Africa. Turning down the chance to run for a third presidential term, he led a safari to collect African fauna for the Smithsonian Institute.

Muir—who had praised Roosevelt, saying of their meeting in Yosemite, "I never before had so interesting, hearty, and manly a companion"—was disappointed in his friend for going on this grand hunting trip. But he didn't take down the photograph of TR that he had hung in his study, and he never disparaged him publicly. Giving him the benefit of the doubt, he believed that the president was doing what he had said he would around their campfire: collect for science.

On the surface, that's exactly what Roosevelt did. His report on his yearlong expedition, *African Game Trails,* contains a biological survey of Mount Kenya, discourses on protective coloration in sub-Saharan fauna, and appendixes listing the taxonomic and common names of the animals he and his zoologists collected. However, in his narrative, TR sheds his scientific dress clothing and uses words such as "fun," "glee," "delight," and "joy" to describe his lion hunting. His bullets "smash lungs," "cut hearts," and "shatter ribs."

Teetering between adolescent bloodlust and his knowledge of approaching scarcities and extinctions (he predicted the demise of the African rhino), he tries to strike a balance between nostalgia and realism. The result sounds like someone who wants to leave an old home but can't find another house to live in.

"We shot nothing that was not used either as a museum specimen or for meat—usually for both purposes," he wrote. "We were in hunting grounds practically as good as any that have ever existed; but we did not kill a tenth, nor a hundredth part of what we might have killed had we been willing."

Along with his son Kermit, he kept a dozen trophies for Sagamore Hill, about which he said, "The making of such a collection is in itself not only proper but meritorious; all I object to is the loss of all sense of proportion in connection therewith." Concentrating on "record heads," as did many of the trophy hunters of his (and this) day, particularly infuriated Roosevelt. He calls it "a craze" and "absurd"; and to point out its shortcomings, he makes this analogy: "It is just as with philately, or heraldry, or collecting the signatures of famous men. The study of stamps, or of coats of arms, or the collecting of autographs, is an entirely legitimate amusement, and may be more than a mere amusement; it is only when the student or collector allows himself utterly to misestimate the importance of his pursuit that it becomes ridiculous."

Muir would never have equated animals with stamps or autographs, and nor could I, even as a boy. I looked up at the Cape buffalo staring down its nose at me and wondered if TR hadn't tried to come to a similar conclusion. Maybe he had, but, ever the political presser of flesh, he hadn't been able to state it with the directness of someone like Muir. Coming home from Africa, he had told his friends that he didn't care if he never fired his rifle again, and increasingly he repeated a theme that he had penned before leaving for his safari.

"More and more," he wrote,

as it becomes necessary to preserve the game, let us hope that the camera will largely supplant the rifle. It is an excellent thing to have a nation proficient in marksmanship, and it is highly undesirable that the rifle should be wholly laid by. But the shot is, after all, only a small part of the free life of the wilderness. The chief attractions lie in the physical hardihood for which the life calls, the sense of limitless freedom which it brings, and the remoteness and wild charm and beauty of primitive nature. All of this we get exactly as much in hunting with the camera as in hunting with the rifle; and of the two, the former is the kind of sport which calls for the higher degree of skill, patience, resolution, and knowledge of the life history of the animal sought.

If this were true, why had he shot so much in Africa, even though he claimed that he hadn't? Why was it so essential to have one last test—to stand before charging lions when he had stood before charging Spaniards and grizzly bears and Indian braves? His sister claimed that TR's near hysterical love of facing danger had to do with his disappointment in their father's having served in mufti during the Civil War. Reluctant to fight against relatives in the South but still wanting to help the war effort, Theodore Senior got himself appointed allotment commissioner by President Lincoln. He traveled to military camps, persuading soldiers to set aside voluntary pay deductions for their families. Young Teddy, however, was unimpressed with his father's nonviolent service. Crushed and bitter that his father hadn't carried a gun, he never hesitated in his own life to pick one up.

A woman in a green national park uniform touched my arm. The museum was closing. I returned the books to the shelves, took a last look at the buffalo head, and rode my bike into the long summer dusk—long as a continent, deep as the world. I was looking for a niche someplace between Theodore and John.

JUST a FISHING WRITER

One evening in Quito, Ecuador, as I walked down a narrow, cobblestone street, I came around a corner and saw a bookstore. In its window were three novels: *Absalom, Absalom!*, by William Faulkner; *The Sun Also Rises*, by Ernest Hemingway; and *U.S.A.*, by John Dos Passos. There was nothing else against the green felt of the window display except a sign that read *Tres autores famosos de los Estados Unidos.*

At the time, I had already sold quite a few essays about fishing and hunting to outdoor magazines, and in fact was working my way through Central and South America by angling, writing about my adventures, and sending the typescripts back to the United States. Sometimes months went by as I ate rice and beans in my VW bus, worked on a novel, and waited for a check, too poor to buy much gas, too rich to leave the beach I was living on.

"An enviable life," a much older writer told me as we drank beer in a seaside bar, which I sometimes called my office. Under my breath, I scoffed at his estimation. For me, writing fishing stories was little better than washing dishes. In my heart, I knew that I was cut out for greater stuff, the stuff staring at me through the window of the foreign-language bookstore in Quito. More than anything else in the world, I wanted to be in that window. I wanted to write serious books, fiction. I was tired of being "just a fishing writer."

Seeing my bearded reflection against the novels, I promised myself that I would be in that window, that I would do everything in my power to live a life that could be converted into fiction. I would never again say that I was a fishing writer, ever. I was a writer, period.

With two friends I had met along the road—Steve, who looked like a tall weather-beaten cowboy, and Bill, who, with his wispy blond beard, looked like an Irish minstrel—I continued south. We were heading for Aconcagua, the tallest mountain in the Western Hemisphere, which we wanted to climb, and toward the Lake District of Chile and Argentina, where I wanted to fish for trout. I reckoned that it was okay for a writer to still fish for trout, just as long as he didn't make it his business to write about it.

We took a bus from Quito to Lima, Peru, followed it with the train up to Ayacucho, and another bus to Cuzco, and another train to Machu Picchu, where we walked among the ruins. Then we sailed across Lake Titicaca, and boarded yet another bus to La Paz, Bolivia, where the electricity and water were intermittent, and the bakers were on strike so there was no bread. From La Paz we took the train across the desert to Antofagasta, Chile, and yet another bus down to the capital, Santiago, where it was the middle of summer, the flowers were in bloom, and the stunning, dark-eyed Chilean women walked around in frocks cut above their knees.

This took us three months, living out of our backpacks and

spending three dollars a day for food, lodging, and transport. It was a time when much was possible with very little money, not because we were young and inured to hardship, but because the stunning places of the world had yet to advertise themselves. We didn't know that we were helping to invent adventure travel or that we were about to run into a moment that we would remember for the rest of our lives.

The *International Herald Tribune* had warned us that things were amiss in Chile, which up until that point had been South America's longest-lived democracy: The country's generals were about to take on its democratically elected Marxist president, Salvador Allende. But we ignored the warnings to stay away. We needed to get to our mountain, and going through Chile was the shortest way there, and, to be truthful, we wanted to see what a coup d'état looked like.

It looked like Swiss cheese, the Hilton hotel and the Presidential Palace riddled with large bullet holes and bomb craters, Salvador Allende already quite dead (his body, in the well-publicized morgue photo, also riddled with bullet holes), and a pretty rude gang of strutting generals in power. Yet with great Latin insouciance, the people of Santiago continued to stroll through the city's parks, to visit the museums, to drink coffee at the sidewalk cafés, to go to movies, and to pack the buses at 10:30 P.M., trying to get home before the eleven o'clock curfew.

We spent our evenings at the Café Monjitas, a stroll across the Plaza Armas from our hotel, where we ate lobster, green salads, and freshly baked baguettes, washing it down with Concha y Toro white wine, all for ninety-seven cents U.S. Hyperinflation had wiped out the savings of the nation, but for three gringos, Chile was the bargain of our young lives.

After dinner, we strolled around the fountains, under the giant leafy trees, talking Spanish to the young women, who giggled behind their hands. Near eleven, we returned to the Hôtel de France, with its balconies and tall windows, the great brass beds and clean white sheets, the endless hot water, all for a dollar a night.

Just after eleven, the air sweet with the scent of jacaranda and the Southern Cross hanging in the dark sky, the volley of machine guns ripped across the town, followed by the screams of those who hadn't made it indoors; then the fires and sirens began.

Amazed and quite honestly thrilled that I was living through a coup d'état, I took careful notes about everything I saw and heard, standing on the balcony at the end of the day and writing by the light of a flashlight. During the day, I searched out people who had been close to Allende, spoke with them, and learned how the CIA had helped the generals along.

For me, this was another wretched confirmation of how the United States couldn't keep its nose out of other nations' affairs, devastating much of what it touched as it tried to make the world safe for democracy with the help of Latin and Asian generals. And I believed that my view of U.S. foreign policy wasn't merely the idealism of a young college graduate who had opposed the Vietnam War. One of my high-school classmates had come back from Vietnam in a body bag; another returned a lifelong cripple; the brother of my closest fishing buddy in college had disappeared in his plane along the Cambodian border and was one of those who were never found—not a dog tag, not a dental filling, not even a rumor.

No foreign policy, no manifesto to contain communism (which I hadn't gauged as much of a threat to democracy as my elders did), was worth these costs. But others gauged costs and benefits differently, which I learned in no uncertain terms when

I came back through Santiago a few months later. Some of the people with whom I had spoken had disappeared. When I asked about them, people shrugged. One man, with enormous dark eyes and white hair, quietly closed his front door in my face. By then, too, I had learned the shape of the game.

Food for our mountain trip packed, we were set to head into Argentina, but first decided to spend an afternoon swimming at Viña del Mar, one of Chile's Pacific resorts. We stopped in Valparaíso along the way, the nation's major seaport, and bought some fruit, cheese, and bread in a market. Strolling to a park, we laid out our picnic. We had an hour to wait for the next bus up the coast.

I had just bit into my peach when I felt the muzzle of a rifle touch the side of my face.

Steve and Bill looked up as two other soldiers, young and nervous, pointed automatic rifles at them and a colonel waved a service revolver in the general direction of all of us. I remember thinking that the rifles were M-14s and that the soldiers had their fingers on the triggers and their safeties off.

"Whoa," said Bill, stopping in the midst of spreading some cheese on his bread.

The soldiers, unsure about what to do now, looked across the park to a fire station around whose entrance were two machine guns, surrounded by sandbags. The machine guns were trained on us, and to the side of each gunner was a soldier holding a belt of cartridges. In the door between the machine guns appeared a heavyset man with short black hair and a beige suit. Surveying the scene, he shouted, "¡Tírelos!"

"What did he say?" said Bill, whose Spanish was poor.

Taking the peach from my mouth, I said, " 'Shoot them.' "

The colonel gestured with his revolver and yelled, "Get up."

He jerked the barrel toward the fire station. With guns in the smalls of our backs and our hands over our heads, our picnic left behind, we marched inside.

The colonel led us into a room. He sat us down on a bench, took our passports, and slapped them on his hand.

"Don't you know that any three people congregating in a public place is considered an illegal demonstration against the new government?"

We did not.

"There are hundreds of people walking around in Santiago," I said.

"*¡Eso es Valparaíso!*" he shouted. (This is Valparaíso!). He added that the city was the hotbed of the *Resistencia,* the forces still loyal to Allende.

Surprisingly, there wasn't real anger in his voice. He actually seemed embarrassed by the whole affair and couldn't look us in the eye. Then he glanced at the door. The heavyset man in civilian clothes jerked his thumb down the hall. The three soldiers who were still guarding us motioned with their rifles. We walked down a set of stairs and into a basement corridor, without windows. At its end was a cinder-block wall.

They put the guns at the back of our heads. Steve was on my left, Bill on my right. I tried to look at them, but the civilian barked, "*Anden.*" Walk.

I did and I thought, *I was biting into a peach on a sunny day by the Pacific Ocean just minutes ago and now I'm almost dead.*

My notebook was in my back pocket, but I didn't think about all the books I would now never write. I didn't think of my family or the girlfriend whom I had left behind to go traveling. I didn't think of my old dog with whom I had grown up. I didn't revisit, in a flash, all the wonderful times I had had in the mountains and on the ocean. All I thought about was having peach juice sticky on my chin and that this was a stupid way to die and how ridiculous it was that, with only seconds left to live, I couldn't think of one significant thing except that I had peach juice on my mouth.

They marched us to the wall so our noses touched it, the muzzles of the rifles pressing into the backs of our heads. I could feel the muzzle shake as the soldier behind it trembled violently. They held us there for a few eternal seconds . . . then turned us around . . . and marched us back upstairs and sat us down on the bench.

The heavyset man, his dark jowls shaking with rage, began to berate us. Didn't we know this wasn't the United States, that this was a country at war, that we couldn't come here with all our ideas about freedom and expect to just run around. Obviously we were *socialistas,* perhaps even *revolucionarios* come to make more trouble. He jabbed a finger into Bill's chest, and Bill, now recovered from the deflation of almost being executed, jumped up and jabbed a finger back into the chest of the heavy man.

Steve and I tackled him, sitting him down.

Livid, the heavy civilian screamed at Bill that he would have him shot on the spot.

"*Oiga,*" I said, listen, and opened my arms in an apologetic gesture. "We're sorry we broke the martial law here in Valparaíso. But we're anything but *socialistas.* We're just *andinistas,* come to climb Aconcagua, and *pescadores* as well, fishermen, come to angle in the Lake District." Sincere tone. Friendly. Chamber of commerce. Wasn't it all about commerce, anyway?

"All my life, since I've been a *muchacho,*" I held my hand about three feet off the ground. "I've read about the Lake District, and about Patagonia, and I've come all this way to write about your country for my magazine. *Soy solamente una periodista de la pesca.* I'm *just* a fishing writer, who has come all this way to write about your beautiful country and its large trout." *Las truchas grandes.*

I was on a roll now. Later, I turned queasy at how bold I was.

"Besides," I said, "we're going to meet our friends from the American Embassy at Viña for lunch, and we're already two hours late. They know we came through Valparaíso, and they will come looking for us."

This was a lie.

But it made the colonel send the heavyset man a glance, as if to say, "You see, more trouble now."

I was going to say that the ambassador was a personal friend, but I thought that would be pushing our luck. So I tried something that could be verified.

"If you want some proof of who we are, let's call my editor in *Nueva Yorke.* Here's the number." I picked up a pencil and wrote on a scratch pad. "He'll tell you that I'm *solamente una periodista de la pesca.*"

I'm *just* a fishing writer.

"¡Carajo!" said the heavyset man with disgust and a trace of disappointment, as if he were being cheated. He picked up our passports in frustration and threw them back on the desk.

"Maricones," he spat, faggots, and stalked out.

The colonel picked up the passports and waved them before us. "This isn't the United States," he shouted halfheartedly. "We have our rules."

"Absolutamente," I said, tentatively reaching out my hand. (Just give me those passports, you mother . . .) "And promise, we'll be out of Valparaíso on the next bus, by taxi if you want."

My hand extended a little farther.

"Vayan rapidos," he said, handing me our passports.

"Como el viento." Like the wind.

We ran out the doors and toward the bus station.

Across the aisle from each other, Steve on one side, Bill and I on the other, we sat silently, in a daze, watching the ocean go by.

Finally, Bill said, "What did you say to him?"

"I said that our friends from the American Embassy were waiting for us in Viña and that they would ask questions."

"I got that part. Pretty good. Before that."

"Oh, I said we were climbers and fishermen, not revolutionaries, and that we were here only to see their beautiful country. And that I was . . . just a fishing writer."

"You nearly got us killed," Steve said to Bill.

"He pissed me off."

"I thought you were going to stab him with your finger," I said to Bill, and, for the first time in hours, I felt a smile on my face.

We looked at the red and yellow houses of Viña approaching, the sun low behind them, turning the ocean gold. I could still feel the spot where the muzzle of the rifle had pressed against my skull, like a hat worn too long. I watched the approaching boardwalk full of strolling women in summer dresses and the umbrellas shading the seaside tables where couples sat, eating lobster and drinking wine. The smoke from the grills went up toward the sky, and suddenly, life was about as sweet as I had ever known it, sweeter than in any mountain range or on any trout river, even if I had admitted that I was . . . *just* a fishing writer.

A LAKE DISTRICT LETTER

Dear H., back there in the States—

Hitching on a hard dirt road, sunbaked, the prints of horse hooves along its shoulders. A broad river winds up a yellow valley—Wyoming wide, Holsteins dotted on it. The mountains rise bare, brown, snowcapped, flotillas of white clouds sailing through their passes. So pretty my eyes purse as if they had taste buds that just had gotten a hit of something sweet.

Sitting on my *mochila*, my pack, on the side of the road, waiting for a ride, I write, hearing my thoughts finding a language someplace between English and Spanish. *Sé que amo esta vida andanda.* I know I like this walking life.

These days, the Spanish sounds more like how I feel, walking across the country, stretching out, loose and easy. Thirteen months gone from the States, half of it camping out—I feel as if the southern landscape has osmosed into my spine and its language into my head. I feel *lleno*, full, of the country's music.

And I'm happy (wow, what a concept), and with some surprise watch myself on this road, waiting patiently and feeling decent instead of guilty. Maybe actually living with the people of the Third World has made me realize that they really don't want our help, at least not in the way that we've given it. Nor do they have much use for the words I thought I would write that would become a positive force to overturn the injustices of the world. They want to be treated without paternalism, which means reducing one's stature. With kids that means not talking down to them. With the folks of the world it means getting down in the dirt.

I think of you, receiving this letter in your office in the basement of the philosophy building, its gray stone covered by ivy; of the quad where I gave up my draft card and where we debated for hours about which was more valuable: to go to jail for one's convictions or to leave and use the freedom to learn, to teach, to change. It never was a real choice for me, H. The thought of being incarcerated, of losing the sky and rivers, was too much to bear, a cost too high to pay to protest this insane war.

And even though I'm glad that I helped in the scream—telling Them that thought wasn't dead—I've run out of the energy for shouting. I look up toward the northern horizon and still see the United States roaring through the world, supporting dictators, mowing down forests, you and your new batch of young men and women now more than likely agonizing over Watergate and the ecocrisis. Maybe things will change, and I'll get back into the fray, but right now I feel distant from it all, distant and buffered, and wanting to see some of the planet before it gets turned into the developed world's notion of a suburban paradise.

The Northern Hemisphere, its industrial noise and addiction to oil, have fallen with the Dipper; Pinochet, his machine guns and curfews, are safely behind the Andes; and Perón, balancing his pro- and antiguerrilla forces, is far away across the Pampas.

Here, under an unsmogged Crux, the world is at peace with it-self and I with my soul.

It's been a slow devolution, a sinking back, oddly enough achieved through climbing, through going up, which I guess is the overview I craved, and the proof, the love, and the purity I sought when I left the States. High up, in the thin air of the planet's skin, one's every motion slows down, just as one's travel does in the less developed world. Being poor has also helped me to understand the value of slowness. I came south overland slowly and inexpensively—hitching, taking buses, walking—and watched the land change under my feet, learning, without a choice in the matter, the value of patience and the elegance of unfilled time: diurne to nocturne . . . summer to autumn . . . the sun shadowing yet another degree of latitude, slow pendulum between Cancer and Capricorn. I feel centuries old and con-nected to the stones' passing and the rivers' flow.

Fishing, too, has changed for me, going from a sport, an ac-cumulation of species and records and places, to a meditation on home. Casting has become the mantra that connects me to the water planet, the miracle of immersion in free-flowing rivers, and to trout, the rivers' flowered gifts, measuring our souls. They're really too pretty to kill, but, when killed to eat, they explain who we are: appetites within the minds of angels.

And this is the way it has been the last few days, when I seemed to see the top and the bottom clearly at last and felt the need to write to you.

Yesterday it blew, sometimes raining, as the wind ripped at the hut, its walls shaking, the guy wires humming. We ate sardines and bread, drank tea, hung out, and read. Steve, tall and lanky, lay on one bunk; Bill, slight and blond, lay on another; I was on the third. Head to feet, head to feet, head to feet around the table of stoves and canned goods. Three *vagabundos* on the side of an Andean mountain, waiting for a break in the weather.

One at a time, we went to the door, watched the sky, returned, talked about the route—the many crevasses that we needed to skirt and the possibility of falling into them and dying. I sometimes wonder why I have bound up so many months of my journey with these two people. They are the only two whom I've met who in some way risk their lives for an uncommon purity, for a cleansing that leaves behind so much dross. Steve went voluntarily to Vietnam. Bill, like me, stayed behind. Yet the three of us came out of the war years with a similar conclusion: Better to go to your death because you and not some government, with its ever-shadowed motives, have chosen it.

As the evening deepened, we watched the stars appear. The wind had lost its force, the glacier fell away thousands of feet from the foot of the hut, and I felt like an old flier or an eagle. In a very quiet way—a distant rockslide rumbling, the melt lisping over nearby rocks, the candlelight sputtering—I also felt what it means to be a hero. It has nothing to do with being brave. It has to do with moving through the country humbly; facing the risks it gives you with patience; waiting for calmer weather and returning another day; becoming like a fish or a bird, who moves swiftly but without challenge or anger.

This morning, we climbed quickly, Bill kicking steps and leading through the crevasses up the steep snow slopes. Stopping in a safe nook under some ice cliffs, we ate and drank, then unroped and scrambled up the black, snow-covered rocks and over fingers of translucent ice.

Beyond the cliffbands, we tied into the rope again and scaled a steep wall of névé, Bill plunging in his ax and kicking steps, showers of ice needles and balls of snow raining upon me, my avalanche upon Steve; the red double rope spiraling up into the heaven where the ice met the sky in a clear white line. I could see the bottom of Bill's crampons and the top of Steve's head, his grin flashing under his blue balaclava. Behind him, below him, the glacier plummeted away to the distant pine-covered hills . . . green valleys . . . smoky green lakes, the clouds quicksilver and violet puffs, the horizon the Pampas and the Pacific.

The rope lifted, breaking sheets of ice that the wind caught and tossed away. Bill shouted something lost in the upward fall of sky—something pulling, stretching, uplifting. Roped between these two friends, climbing upward, I felt born again, shouting labor's birth sound—half cry, half laugh, pushing so much joy into the bright new world that death vanished. Born again, my arms wrapping around the heaving shoulders of the sky, I felt a parent to myself.

We clambered over the top of the ice cliff. Was it a false summit? The snow slope fell away, and the other side of the hidden earth appeared, the horizon curved and twelve thousand feet below us, the planet recently created, as were we.

Now a stream rushes over a rocky bed and the flames of the campfire snap softly as the wind rises and falls. The western sky is violet, our mountain standing above the trees, its cone of ice pulling my eye. Just a few hours ago, we stood there.

Glissading and downclimbing, we came all the way to earth in an afternoon, camping in these pines by a long turquoise lake, not putting up the tent because the sky was so clear. After laying out our boots and rope to dry, Steve and I walked along the lake to its outlet to fish while Bill stayed behind and read. A stump stood at the outlet, parting the exiting water slightly as it flowed over a rock spillway, the water opal and amber colored because of the cobbled bottom. The current made a slow deep whoosh as it passed the broken-off log.

On the third toss, I saw a fish wriggle out of the depths beneath the stump and grab my lure. I struck, he rolled on the surface and vaulted, a rainbow against the smoky gray towers on the opposite lakeshore. After several minutes, I pinned him on the sand, knocked him on the head, and lifted him by the gills, an enormous male rainbow trout with a hooked jaw, glistening with green and violet spots.

As I cleaned the fish, Steve jogged back to make a fire. When I was done, I saw Bill approaching. We walked back together, Bill carrying my rod and I the fish, its tail scraping the sand. The sun was gone now and a low bank of cumulus floated where it had disappeared. Five gold ducks flew into the purple clouds and vanished.

Bill and I walked up the beach slowly, not wanting the evening to end. All the mountains of Argentina seemed to surround the lake, and really they were the mountains of our home, the Rockies, coming all the way down here to meet us, to meet our hard ice mountain that we had wished to climb and had, hurting no one else in the process, and had come back from.

The night smell was coming fresh and fast, and frogs began to sing. Bill said, "It is really sad to go back." But even as he said it, we knew that we would all go. Steve first, Bill second, and I, who was the least held to a job, last. But I, too, would go. There are only a few places in the world that are really home.

We continued up the beach, the night smell rising from the grass, and a full gold moon rising in the crotch of the hill. We sat on a grassy bank and watched it, having no destination except our dinner, and that could wait. Finally we walked to camp, where Steve's fire glimmered through the pines. We laid the trout on a beat-up wire grill that we carried, and we crouched over its fillets, sizzling with lemon and butter. In a few minutes, we ate them, along with crackers and raisins because that was all the food we had left.

Now my friends are asleep and the Southern Cross hangs in an open spot in the trees as I write to you. The wood burns quietly and smells of flowery vanilla perfume; the air smells of earth that has been washed by a long, long rain. By the embers of the fire, I am so tired. It's been such a long, long trip, H. Strange, how much longer it takes to make peace than war.

Take care, my friend.

Tu amigo en la tierra austral

P.S.—This was one of those letters that are written and somehow never sent. No envelope, no stamps, no post office. It was closed in a journal and found and reread years later when I wanted to remember what it was like—exactly, in the words of the time—to grow up in a time when my friends, as young and hopeful as myself, died in a war, killed others in a war, that I could not understand and still cannot make sense of.

I looked for it because this week, over two decades from when the letter was written, I saw these friends' faces in the black marble of their monument, of the monument of our times, along with my own reflected image. I had spent the day listening to the Senate Energy and Natural Resources Committee hearings, just up the Mall, on the issue of selling more timber off our national forests. I guess I couldn't stay out of the fray all that long.

I went to the monument because I had also heard my friends' voices, a great babble of them, repeating why they had to go to Vietnam, or why they left for Canada, or why they became conscientious objectors, or why they got 4-Fs. I heard all our voices, mixing in anger, as I listened to Robert McNamara's voice on National Public Radio, talking about his new book, and how he knew that the war was unwinnable, but he did nothing to make that knowledge public, did nothing to help us make one of the most important decisions of our and our families' lives.

It was such a triumphant and dismal feeling of validation to be in Washington, D.C., this week, among the heraldic buildings that emanate so much power and confidence, to be on the very streets where I was once teargassed, to stand before my friends who are now ashes and black marble, and to hear the former secretary of defense recant.

I wish, I wish, I wish that it could all be changed, and that I wouldn't have to know that as young people some of us were really right and that he and the rest of our elders were really wrong, and that going off to catch some trout and climb some mountains, while our nation called us traitors was no traitorous act at all but a saner form of allegiance. I wish that those who were intent on saving Vietnam could have known what many still do not know now: that there is a difference between what we call a nation and what we call our home.

THE BACK BEND

Sunday. Sore from the previous day's climb, we sit on the deck and watch the cirrostratus bloom over the Tetons, promising rain by the afternoon. Down from Montana, Ed and Nancy are interested in finding some equine property. Chrislip, my climbing partner and on holiday between consulting jobs, will be heading back to Colorado soon. Touched by having three old friends visit at the same time, I momentarily indulge myself and imagine this northwestern corner of Wyoming as the center of the continent.

But after three pots of coffee, Ed and Nancy saddle up their Volvo and return to Bozeman, and Chrislip goes into Jackson on an errand. Left with an abyss of unstructured time, I drift by the study's bookshelves—too filled with other people's emotions—and gravitate to the back room where most of my time structurers lay: the road bike, the climbing and kayaking gear, and my fishing rods.

Gathering waders and vest, I hesitate a moment over the choice of rod and finally pick the two-weight, which at one and a half ounces is so light and effortless in the hand that it rarely colors a day astream with purpose. In fact, throwing line with its taut eight-foot length reminds me more of blowing bubbles than of anything so scientific as duping a smart creature like a trout with a bit of feather and flotsam.

At the eastern border of Grand Teton National Park, the Gros Ventre River turns away from the road, recedes behind a swell of spruce-covered hills, and runs incognito for several miles before reemerging as a rocky channel behind the Teton Valley Ranch, our small settlement, and my house.

Few anglers fish this back bend, because to reach it one must wade the Gros Ventre above a small rapid that tumbles directly into a band of cliffs that guard a deep green pool. Even after you've studied the crossing through Polaroid glasses and have chosen the shallowest line, the ford can be waist-deep, and the current is strong. The unfit and the timid usually turn back here.

Most days, I am neither. Still, I have never much liked swimming in fast rivers. Therefore, going with the flow, using my rod as a staff, and treading over the rocks with care, I quarter downstream, reach the other side without incident, and walk a gravel bar to the pools below the cliffs. Just as I pause and survey the pools, the sun emerges from the bank of lowering clouds and spreads a rich tannic light across the bottom.

Prospecting, I turn stones over in the shallows and find them teeming with the small black cases of *Trichoptera* caddis fly larvae, the second stage of the four stages—egg, larva, pupa, and adult—that take this insect from birth to death.

Most anglers, including myself, have resisted the intrusion of this sort of entomological language into casual excursions. Yet mastery of a task has always produced a specialized vocabulary. As I've become more sophisticated in matching the insect life of rivers with imitations, a bit of Latin has become part of my workaday language. I have friends, though, who find taxonomic language pretentious, stating that it's no more than another symptom of the complex lives we live. To them, I can only say that immersion in a home always produces such lexicons. Witness the Inuit, who have scores of words for what most of us can call no more than "snow."

Holding the larvae in my palm, I remember a fishing text informing me that *Trichoptera* has about nine hundred species. Feeling inadequate, I guess that this is the genus *Limnephilus*, whose larvae form thick tubular cases of stone and sand around themselves. Hoping that the trout aren't as fastidious as my old Latin teacher and some other fishermen I know, I tie on two small black flies—one that I bought in New Zealand a couple of years ago and whose name I can no longer remember and one called simply a pheasant tail. Both somewhat resemble the larvae on the river's stones.

Those unfamiliar with fly-fishing may find this grubbing about on the bottom of a river while mumbling Latin flummery a bit disconcerting and certainly not in keeping with the classic view of the fly angler dropping a lovely winged imitation delicately on the surface of a placid stream dimpled by the rings of rising trout. Yet just as most of us eat toast rather than croissants most mornings, so too do trout, day in and day out, eat more of these plebeian nymphs and larvae than flying insects, especially in a cold climate like this one, where insect hatches come late in the spring and end early in the fall. Those skilled in plumbing the depths of a river with these homely flies take far more fish on far more days than those who hope to lure a trout to the surface for a dramatic strike.

Tackle rigged, I wade across a submerged bar and into a deep pool bordered by cliffs. Wild roses grow on ledges above me, and their bright pink petals turn in the eddies at the base of the rocks.

I'm bargaining that the pool is home to *Salmo clarki*, the native trout of the Rockies and my home fish. Named for the reddish-orange slash that extends along each side of its lower jaw, the cutthroat has an olive back, a yellow belly, and a pale hint of cranberry along its sides, upon which are scattered black spots. As it happens, the cutthroat's common name is a more accurate physical description than *Salmo*, which means to leap and which the fish rarely does, and *clarki*, after Captain William Clark of "Lewis and," who, like all those individuals who have been honored by having their name given to a species, merely happened upon a creature whose existence antedated that of its discoverer by millennia.

As a sport fish, the cutthroat gets mixed reviews. Those who enjoy catching numerous fish for the pan enjoy it. Those who are used to the challenge of rainbows or browns find the cutthroat omnivorous and gullible. In fact, a study in Yellowstone National Park found that wild cutthroat trout were twice as catchable as wild brook trout (and brookies who live in the West are known for their stupidity) and about eighteen times as catchable as that intellect of the salmonids, the brown trout. Nonetheless, in the pan, few fish can rival the orange-meated sweetness of a cutthroat, and with respect to the aesthetics of the wild, few sights can match this muted-orange and yellow-green fish swirling close to your net as you stand knee-deep in a stream far from the road.

As I begin to cast upstream, swallows sweep from the cliffs, twittering speedy songs. A slow processional of puffy clouds float overhead, from dark canyon rim to the opposite, sun-illumined mountainside, and the breeze makes crescent-shaped patterns of tiny riffles on the pool, as if a scythe were mowing the water. Into just such a bit of erectile current, I drop my lure, my object being to have it tumble freely near the bottom. I've added a pair of tiny split shot to the ten-foot leader to make sure this happens—enough weight to take the flies down to the rocks but not enough to snag them.

Of course, if the water is deep the resultant and hoped-for action is sometimes invisible. This is the case today, and I can only keep a careful eye on the end of my fly line. Any sudden twitch or dart downward can mean that the split shot has bounced over a rock or that a fish has taken the fly.

On the third drift, the fly line darts, I lift the rod, and a steady throbbing pressure indicates that a *Salmo* has taken one of my nymphs. The trout makes one fast run downstream, no more than a few feet, before shaking the hook that, because I release most of my fish, is barbless.

I throw another cast upstream and within the first ten feet of drift hook another cutthroat who runs the length of the pool, flashes near the surface twenty yards from me, then sulks on the bottom. Walking downstream, I recover line, pleased with the heaviness of the fish. Two more runs tire it, and as I crank the leader into the guides and reach with my landing net, I feel the sinking emptiness that comes when one's expectations aren't met by reality.

The fish that struggles in the net is *Prosopium williamsoni*, the mountain whitefish. Widely distributed in the western United States and native to the headwaters of the Missouri River basin, the whitefish has a tubular body lacking elegance of line. It also has a short head, an overhanging snout, a blunt and suckerlike mouth, and a uniformly whitish-green color highlighted by a single pink blush on its gill plates, which isn't dermal pigmentation but gills showing through the transparent gill cover.

The whitefish takes almost every fly that a trout will, fights well, and grows larger than most of its riverine neighbors. In fact, the specimen in my hand is twenty inches long. On most streams in the United States, a twenty-inch trout is greeted by shouts by all except the most incurably blasé. Yet I place the fish back in the river with no more than a disappointed sigh.

Perhaps if *Prosopium*, which means "small mask," had a nose job, or could only visit the Ralph Lauren shop of the piscatory world and get some pastels to liven up its drab business white, anglers would like it more, for even when you can catch many of them, they never seem to satisfy.

This callous fact is brought home with ever more certainty as I work up through the pool and take whitefish after whitefish. I stop counting after one dozen. Yet I can't bring myself to leave. The perfume of the rose petals, the cavorting of the swallows, the gentle wind blowing the willows, are too lovely to abandon—and also I wish that I could catch a trout so as to infuse a final element of harmony into the scene.

But no trout touches my fly. I abandon the pool and walk downriver, hoping to leave the whitefish behind. Purple asters sprinkle the banks, while that prettiest of all gilias, the red *Gilia aggregata*, shares the grass with harebell, pale and innocent as an arctic sky, and with some lavender clover. The path through the flowers has been made by deer. After a short walk, I descend to the ankle-deep water and scout the rapids and pools ahead, where the river falls in an S-shaped bend.

Taking another step, I start and jump back. At my feet is a snake, two feet long and writhing. Its ugly, misshapen head sprouts four green eyes and two pectoral fins.

Leaning forward gingerly, I see that I haven't discovered a new four-eyed monster, but a copper-colored garter snake, jaws agape around the nearly swallowed torso of a mottled sculpin.

The sculpin, which resembles a catfish, has thick rubbery lips, and a wide, flattened head with eyes on top. Its ventral fins stick from the corners of the snake's jaws, and the snake's eyes, distorted backward as it tries to swallow the fish, peer at me with a cold, malignant light. It thinks I'm going to steal its dinner, which it probably caught with some stalking and stealth, for sculpins live under stones and logs, and are fairly spry little fish. Or perhaps the sculpin was snoozing.

In any case, "snake eats sculpin" isn't an uncommon riverside event, yet this one-inch-wide snake attempting to eat a two-inch-wide fish—both bug-eyed, straining, gagging, and gulping—turns this ordinary act of survival into a scene so voracious, gluttonous, and disgusting as to be almost pornographic.

I am unable to avert my eyes. I want to see more and follow the snake downstream, where, trying to elude me, it wedges itself between two rocks. I reach down, grasp it behind its head, and in three heaving belches it vomits up the intact sculpin, its dorsal fin somewhat frayed.

The fish falls on a flat rock, takes a spasmodic gasp, and lies still. Feeling that I've interfered with an event in which I had no business, I place the snake back in the river and innocently expect it to return to its prey. But it swims off five cautious feet and watches me. In the meantime, red ants have begun to march from the willows next to the rock. A few walk over the sculpin and, within seconds, communicate by their hurried motions that dinner has arrived. Hordes race from the shore and swarm over the limp fish.

I retire to the bank and watch. The garter, a smart fellow when all is said and done, keeps its beady little eye directly on mine and won't move. After fifteen minutes, I decide that I want to fish for cutthroats more than see who wins the sculpin. I walk on downstream, where the cumulus clouds have built and blackened.

Lightning flickers on the far hillsides, but I reckon that the hits are still far enough away for safety. I drop casts into the pools and catch whitefish in every one. Soon my standing in the river with an eight-foot rod waving in the air while lightning draws closer seems like a truly poor idea, so I walk downriver on the bank until a deep and slowly moving pool appears around the next bend. A rock juts into its depths, and, still hoping that the lightning will pass to the north, I clamber onto the rock and cast. The wind has picked up, rain smites the water, and a loop of my fly line catches around the butt of my rod. As I untangle it—in this moment totally devoid of skill—a fish strikes. Releasing the line from the butt, I set the hook and feel a vehemence that I haven't felt in any of the strikes I've received during the afternoon. The fish runs off fifty feet of line into the center of the river, broaches, and by its pink sides and flash of orange I know that, at last, I've hooked a cutthroat.

I follow downstream as it angrily takes line from the reel, leaps, cartwheels, and slugs it out for all its worth. Of course, it doesn't know I'm going to release it.

And perhaps I won't even get it to the net. The two-weight rod isn't a winch, and the 5X tippet is closer to sewing thread than fishing line, which is why if you land a big fish on this ultralight tackle you get to wear an imaginary campaign ribbon on your chest for the next few weeks.

Frankly, the campaign ribbons grow with every minute that the fight continues. Each run indicates that this isn't a twelve-incher, or even a fifteen-incher. Once, as I get the trout close and see its olive back glimmer two yards from me, it appears husky and perhaps twenty inches long. It could weigh three pounds. Then it dashes from sight, taking another forty feet of line.

Wind spits aspen leaves across the current. Thunder rolls down the valley. The surface of the stream is alive with pelting drops. In the midst of the storm, for just a second or two, I suddenly imagine keeping the trout and broiling it with all the pomp it deserves. I could serve it on a tray, for some friends to whom I've promised a fish dinner, along with the Chardonnay that lies on the cool bottom shelf of one of the kitchen cabinets. And I suddenly hear my internal voice say, "Please, let me land this fish."

It takes another few minutes to work the tiring trout to the net where, its broad tail over the rim, it lunges mightily and the fly—that tiny black imitation of *Limnephilus*—flies freely into the rain. No line breakage, no poor technique, only a quirk of fate—and fishing with a barbless hook—lets the fish escape.

As the rain tapers to a close and the thunder disappears to the east, I continue to cast, but I can't raise a strike, not even from a whitefish. Hooking the fly into the rod butt, I begin walking up- stream on the deer trail that I descended. When I break into a clearing, I spy a tawny shoulder on its farther edge and two tiny fawns leaping in the wet grass. No more than a few days old, they take springing leaps as their little white flags dart like the wings of swifts. The mother whitetail, sensing that a still form has ap- peared in the clearing, raises her head and watches me while her twins jump about her and nuzzle her belly for milk. Then with the solemnity of a queen, she walks into the forest.

Angling back to the river, I aim for the spot where the garter snake vomited its prey upon a rock. Recollecting the start with which I first witnessed the four-eyed monster, I also can't help but wonder if a fishing vest full of carefully tied flies, a one-and- a-half-ounce graphite rod, and a funeral of dill and Chardonnay can make the end any better for a trout than a sculpin.

The stone where the fish lay lies perfectly bare—no sign of prey, or snake, or ants. Could those Lilliputian hordes have dragged the sculpin off? Did the snake return for its rightful catch? Or, by some miracle, could the sculpin have resuscitated itself and flopped back into the river?

No answer presents itself except the silent pool, rose petals on its surface, shivering in the wind.

THE PREACHER of TROUT POKING

Just as some churchgoers sing hymns about salvation each and every Sunday morning, never noticing that the purpose of religion is to help us connect with the essential spirit of the universe, so some anglers learn about bivisibles and midges, double hauls and shooting heads, emergers and spent wings without ever getting down to the fact that standing in a river and waving a pole in the air is all about *catching* trout.

Every once in a while, though, it's refreshing to run into someone who gets to the heart of the matter, who has fish fire in his soul.

Early in the morning the phone rings, and I hear Paul Bruun's bray. A man of superlatives and many appointments, he says quickly, "I'm busy all day, but I got to tell you that I just read the first part of your book and the story about Argentina is stunning. It's the best fishing story ever written."

Thinking of a couple of fishing stories by Hemingway, a novel by Norm Maclean, and another by Herman Melville, I let the comment slide.

"We got to get together," says Paul, a professional fishing guide in Jackson Hole, a columnist for the local paper, and a walking who's who of the sportfishing world.

"How's tomorrow?" I suggest.

We make a date to meet in town, and as we're about to sign off, Paul adds, "Oh, I should tell you. I may have a client, so I might not show up."

He doesn't.

Two weeks go by without a word from Paul. By reading his column in the local paper, I discover that he's been on British Columbia's Babine River, steelhead fishing. In the accompanying photo, he holds a fourteen-pound sea-run rainbow. At least he's had a good reason for not calling. And I really have no reason to complain. I've been up on the Lewis, catching spawning browns.

One night I come home to Paul's voice on my answering machine. "I'm all screwed up in a city council meeting. Call me tomorrow morning."

I do, about eight. "I was on the Babine," he begins, then rattles off a number of rivers whose names would leave any angler envious. He adds, "I got a client on the South Fork tomorrow. Why don't you come?" Before I can accept or beg off, he says, "It's a pigpen down there. Honest. Jaws. And besides I got some new peppers for lunch. You'll love 'em."

"I'll go," I throw in.

"I am sure," he says definitively, "that we can find some trout to entertain you."

Now, what I like about Paul is that, unlike me, he not only thinks about catching trout, but most of the time he actually does it. In fact, when it comes to the celestial ordering of trout anglers, I am in the lower ranks where the young, the dumb, the foolish, and the glaucomic trout sometimes lose their way, while

Paul is up on the gleaming altar of anglerhood. The thought of actually going out with him, that this archangel might tell me some secrets and anoint a fly or two with some of his Tru-Float Goop, leaves me aglow.

Sending a vile-looking stream of Red Man tobacco juice into the blue shore current of the Snake River, not far from where we've launched the boat, he stares at the nine-foot leader I pull off my rod and says, "I won't tell you what to do, but I'd cut that back to three feet."

"How can I tie my tippet onto that fat butt?"

"Get rid of the tippet," he says curtly. "Just tie that mother right here." He points to one of the midsections, which must test about ten pounds.

I feel as if someone has slapped me in the face. The tapered leader is the foundation of fly-fishing. It's above Paul Bruun. It's the Father, the Son, and the Holy Ghost. It's indivisible.

"Look," says Bruun, pursing his mouth under his Stetson and Polaroids. "When a fish chomps this"—he holds up a streamer as big as some of the trout I've caught this summer—"he's not going to concern himself with whether your tippet is 1X or 4X. It's a hog trough out there. And besides, you can fish these big flies better on a short leader."

Bruun wears a pair of neoprene waders and a blue pile jacket. A collapsible sawband landing net is strapped tightly around his waist and sticks up from the small of his back like a dagger. He's a couple of inches over six feet tall, with a lean square jaw and an ample middle. He wears no fishing vest, but in his boat, spread around his command seat, are boxes of flies and, piled along one of the gunwales like ordnance, cased fly rods and reels. The Mackenzie boat, a dory-shaped river runner, has the slim, no-

nonsense readiness of an assault craft, and Bruun, with his bandanna tied around his neck, and the stampede strings of his Stetson loosely coiled on its brim, has the tight, big, powerful look of a general.

"Try that short leader," he advises again.

Remembering something about God sending curve balls to Abraham, I cut it back, make a cast, and discover that indeed the big streamer sails out cleanly on the short piece of mono.

"Too much sidearm on your cast!" Paul yells to me, managing to add, "That double haul is just a way of throwing longer mistakes."

Shouting on the stream? Izaak Walton must be turning over in his grave.

Sending a sharp glance upriver, Paul hollers "Come back" to Steve, the "client" and the manager of the food services at the ski area. Steve's wife has given him a gift certificate for a float with Paul. Built like a linebacker, Steve is waist-deep in the Snake and tossing his fly out into the fast-moving water that tails into the pool I'm fishing.

"You're walking over fish!" shouts Paul. He looks at me and says, "Hey, that's a good poke. You laid it out there. Okay, there's nothing here. Let's go."

I've made only a half-dozen casts, but we get in the boat and set off. Keeping us in the current, Paul spits chew over the side and advises, "Throw it in there." I do and let the fly drift, thinking clearheaded thoughts about some calmly finning trout who will shortly spy my streamer floating down the bankside current.

"Rip that mother out of there," commands Paul. "Strip, strip, strip! Too slow. STRIP! Don't let him see it too good. Poke one there. Quick. Other side of the boat. Blast it out of those riffles."

A fourteen-inch cutthroat slams the streamer as if he thought he were a bluefish. I am shocked at his behavior but don't dwell on it, enjoying his fight. Steve also takes one, but we have little time to relish the first fish of the day. Paul beaches the boat and orders us into battle. "Work that confluence, Steve. Ted, run up along the bar and blast a few casts through that pool."

I make two casts, and Paul, lounging on the gunwale of his boat, yells, "Let's go. Nothing here. One of the best holes in the river is just ahead."

Unconsciously, I trot to the boat—trout fishing as an aerobic sport.

Paul lets the boat float down a small run where the river narrows, then rows hard, ferrying us back across a widening pool. To the east, the mountains on the Idaho-Wyoming border are white with snow. The wheat fields of the Swan Valley shed golden light to the sky, and the cottonwoods along the river are bare and yellow. Three Vs of geese fly overhead, honking.

Quietly, Paul says, "Why don't you wade out there and cast?"

The pool is more of a deepening of the big, rangy Snake than an actual pool—a place where the nervous current gets room to stretch left and right but still race.

The lure Paul has given me looks too gaudy to my conservative eye, so I put on a solid black Wooly Bugger as long as my index finger. When wet, it looks like a slimy leech. The wind freshens and blows straight down the river. Both Steve and I are right-handed and the wind, blowing from that side, causes our casts to catch the backs of our vests. Paul rests on the shore—a smooth beach of round dry stones—looking nonchalant.

Steve takes a whitefish, or as Paul sarcastically calls him, "the prince of the river." Nonetheless, this fish with the sucker-shaped mouth is a scrappy fighter and a survivor. Long after the cutthroat and grayling have been wiped out of portions of this, their native range, by angling pressure and the introduction of foreign species, the "prince" lives on. I too catch a whitey then take a few more steps toward the middle of the river and find myself close to belly-button deep. I send a long cast over the tail of the flume, and when the line straightens I strip only once before a great sagging weight comes on to the rod. I plant the hook hard and an orange fish wallows on the surface and runs across the river. Several minutes go by before I can get him close to the shore, where I net him.

Paul bends over the net and says gently, "The small-spotted Snake River cutthroat trout." The fish is orange and pink and luminescent, all mixed with a tint of green, as if every color that has been September has seeped into the river and been captured by this October trout. The fish has also given me a new definition of trout proportions in the Snake.

Do you know those platters used for serving food at truck stops, those oblong ones on which a short-order cook can pile a rib eye and mashed potatoes and still have room for a couple of muffins? Well, this trout's head and tail would have drooped off the ends of such a plate. He is "platter size" and thick.

I release him, stand up, and Paul says, "This hole's got some hogs." He looks at me from under his Stetson and adds, "That was a good fish. Robust."

Steve takes a cutt of about sixteen inches. I take a similar-sized brown. We play in the hole for another hour and move on. Steve has been casting nymphs, and Paul, using his I-don't-want-to-tell-you-what-to-do-but line, has been trying to get him to change to a leech pattern, which seems to be taking more fish. As we approach a confluence in the river where three branches join, Paul, hauling on the oars to get us in position, says again, "I don't want to tell you . . ." This time Steve changes flies.

As we pass an undercut bank where the fast-flowing water swirls into a hole, Paul once again commands, "Drop a poke in there." Steve casts and mends, flipping the line upstream to prevent the fly from dragging unnaturally. "Shit, don't mend!" yells Paul. "You don't need that here. Leave it!"

Steve's rod jerks down. He jerks back and a comfortable bow remains. A dark shape thrashes the surface. "I foul-hooked a whitefish," Steve says, disappointed.

"If you did," says Paul, "you foul-hooked him in the mouth."

The fish takes line downstream. Paul maneuvers the boat to shore and steps out with the net. The trout—we can clearly see its reddish sides—lurches back and forth from the deep water to the shallows, unable to decide where to go. He wears himself out quickly. Steve pumps him closer; Paul nets him on the second try. When Steve holds the brown up for a photo, it's almost as long as Steve is wide—a big male.

Downstream, on a bar designed by MGM (dark cliffs, snow-covered mountains, puffy clouds giving proportion to the sky), we stop for lunch. From two coolers, Paul takes out roast beef sandwiches, potato salad, salami and cheese, half a dozen jars of peppers and pickles, and beer and soft drinks. "Try the Maui sweet onions," he recommends. "Like 'em hot? Try these Cajun ones." After two, I feel as if someone has flicked a Bic in my mouth. But it jazzes me up. I'm ready to run up and down the bank, tossing "pokes" and stripping "blasts" like mad. Maybe this is how Bruun gets his go.

After some stories about the ten- to fourteen-pounders he caught in Argentina last winter (it's almost as if he's giving us a coach's halftime pep talk), we head back to the river. "Left, right, rip, strip, troll." He directs our casts while pulling on the oars and spitting Red Man. For a while we don't score and Paul, scanning the river, says, "What's happened? Eyes. I want to see little faces and eyes. Where are they?"

Nothing does happen for quite a few minutes. We enter a long quiet stretch bordered by cottonwoods. The light has grown warm on the round farm hills, and Paul, staring across the Swan Valley, suddenly blurts out, "I should never teach women how to fish. They go and get married then send me their husbands so I can teach them how to cast. 'Here, Paul,' they tell me. 'I can do nothing with him.'"

We float, we cast. Suddenly, every other throw gets a strike. We work two "pigpens" and a "substructure" and land an ever-increasing tally of fourteen- to sixteen-inch trout.

As we pass an eddy line, Paul yanks on the oars and nods. "There, Ted. Poke one in there."

I look at him. It hardly seems worth a cast. Just a darkening of the river's flow.

"Poke it in there." He motions again with his head.

"Christ! Don't false cast. You are such a wading fisherman. Just throw it."

I throw it.

"Did you see that fish flash?"

"No."

"He did. Poke him again."

Without hesitating, I poke the big gob of Wooly Bugger into the hole, rip it back, and SLAM! An explosion of cutthroat destroys the fly.

The reel handle whirls against my palm, and I hear Paul say, "Nothing like the sound of a $14.95 reel."

He coasts the boat to shore, and I walk along the beach, retrieving the line and feeling the trout's strength in my upraised arm. I bring him to the net five times before he finally surrenders.

Paul lifts him with a dramatic swoop, and I can hardly believe my eyes. He's more brightly colored than my other large cutt— deeper reds and yellows—and bigger. His shoulders are as wide as my palm.

Quietly, as if in the presence of river spirit itself, Paul murmurs, *"Salmo clarki."*

I let *Salmo* go and listen to the October Snake for one moment before Paul says, "Hey, not bad. An okay fish. But just below here there's an awesome pool. Awesome. There are some hogs in there that'll rip you off your feet."

KASHMIRI GAMBIT

On this, my third trip to the Himalaya, I learned to play chess, which was more by default than desire. On my two previous treks, I had entertained the thought of trout fishing. After all, the Himalaya, stretching from Bhutan in the east to the Khyber Pass in the west, is dotted with high lakes as well as being the birthplace of streams so numerous that many remain unnamed, at least on published maps. The names of the great rivers—Imja Kola, Kali Gandaki, Dras, and Braldu—come off the tongue with a sweet sound, like mantras recalling your footsteps long after you have walked up their valleys. I had even gone so far, while looking at maps and planning my treks, to pack in my bags, among the ropes, crampons, and ice-climbing tools, my rod and reel and a box of lures.

All told, on these first two Himalayan walks, I camped out for twelve weeks. I went up rivers and down rivers, crossing them on flimsy plank bridges and also wading them, thigh deep, with my boots tied around my neck. I climbed up to 12,000-foot lakes, to 14,000-foot lakes, to 17,000-foot lakes where there were no lakes at all, only ice. And everywhere I went, not a trout rose. Frequently, this was because the rivers ran heavy with glacial silt. But often the absence of trout was a circumstance of geography, of remoteness. No one had ever made the effort to put trout in most of the eastern Himalaya, an oversight for which the first explorers may be forgiven. When a lake is a twenty-day walk from the roadhead, when the odd helicopter is used to pluck some broken mountaineer from a glacier, when the mountain people carry lowland rice and oranges for a week on their backs over steep, slippery trails, stocking trout takes on a low priority in the round of daily concerns.

Yet like a man who refuses to believe that the beautiful woman he loves really has no heart, I kept searching—up remote cirques to gaze at perfect tarns, through high valleys with bouldery streams, down in the rain forest where waterfalls dropped into granite pools. None had any trout, a state of affairs that left nothing to do with the hours that remained after I had reached camp.

I learned how to play chess. Interesting, but a poor ersatz, and, of course, I still entertained a hope: Among the ice screws, pitons, and magnetic chessboard, I once again tucked a small rod and spinning reel. This time we were going to Kashmir, the northenmost sporting grounds of the old British Raj, a place to which one thoughtful, diligent Victorian, P. J. Mitchell, lt. col., ret., had brought the ova of *Salmo trutta,* the brown trout, in 1901. As an opening, it proved a deep move.

And yet it was one I almost missed. Everything that could have gone wrong did go wrong. We got bumped off our connecting flight from Delhi to Srinagar and spent three frustrating days in the sweltering Indian capital, arguing with airline officials while the thermometer maxed out at 113°F. We had altercations with our trekking company, misunderstandings with our liaison officer, bargaining hassles with the porters, and endless confabulations among ourselves.

When we finally placed a camp at 18,000 feet on the Czech Ridge of Nun Kun and were set to go to its 23,400-foot summit in two grand pushes, it snowed. It didn't snow for five hours or twelve hours or fifteen hours. It snowed for twenty-two hours. And when it stopped snowing, the mountain began to avalanche. And when the avalanches stopped, the wind picked up and blew the snow that had fallen in one place to another place, where it accumulated deeper and began to avalanche all over again. Then it snowed for another day, and as we moved up in a whiteout, a slope fractured beneath us but didn't slide.

We ran out of time; we ran out of energy; we ran out of courage—just about in that order—and beat a retreat to Srinagar, with its hot showers, chicken curry, and moonlight floats on Dal Lake, where the the lotus flowers bloom. The balm lasted a day. Everyone wanted to go home. Even I, having seen some color posters in the tourist office that showed a fisherman holding a large brown trout, wanted to go home. Big mountains do that to you. A big mountain on which you've almost bought the farm does that to you even more.

Feeling played out by a long afternoon during which we had argued the merits of returning to the United States or staying for a fishing trek, I left the lunch table and walked back through the houseboat to our room to face my dusty backpacks full of smelly clothes and crumpled candy-bar wrappers. Sticking from the bottom of the pile were also my rod and reel, which seemed forlorn and misplaced. Looking at the mess, I felt that there was only one thing in the world sadder than a pile of worn and dirty gear in a hotel room twelve thousand miles from home—it's that same pile of gear lying on your living-room floor with nothing but failure locked behind its zippers. I took a shower, got a shikara boy to row me into town, and walked through the bazaar to the fisheries office.

Moving a pawn into enemy territory, I walked under a dull brass plaque that said, LICENCES FISHERIES DEPARTMENT. To the left of the entry, two men—one in a black astrakhan, the other in a white Muslim skullcap—slept on each side of a table that held an antique Remington typewriter. The walls were yellowed and two bare bulbs hung from the ceiling among the tangled tentacles of electric wires. In front of the room, at a desk whose varnish was peeling, sat a swarthy man in a cool, algae-green cotton shirt. Behind him stood filing cabinets, piled high with ledgers, and to his side a swiveling fan lifted the papers on which he worked.

Mr. Darya Ali Raza, the licensing director, reached for one of the armory of stamps by his elbow and struck the document before him with a large blue rectangle of wet ink. He then plucked a smaller stamp from the line waiting at his elbow and inserted its cachet in the center of the stamp. He passed the license over a marble inkstand to the small man in front of his desk, who bobbed his head and rushed out.

"Yes," said Darya Ali Raza to the blond man and woman seated at the table in the opposite corner of the room from the sleeping hangers-on. Between them they had a fair cherub of a son. Their Indian booking agent, a thin, voluble man, escorted them to the desk and said that his clients, from the American Foreign Service in Algeria, would like a trout beat.

Raza extended a smooth arm to the row of chairs before his desk, shook hands with the couple—dressed in matching khaki culottes and Bermuda shorts—chucked their young son under the chin and took from atop his file cabinet a book the size of the Gutenberg Bible. He placed the tome on his desk with all the ceremony due its dimensions, opened it, and ran a finger down its many columns.

"There are no beats left," he announced.

"None?" cried the agent.

"None," said Raza.

"Not a one?" said the man.

"None," repeated Raza. "It's high season, you know."

"I find this difficult to believe," said the booking agent.

"Ah," said Raza, turning one of the heavy pages. "Perhaps a beat off the beaten track might be available." He smiled at his pun.

I half closed my eyes, sunk deeper into my chair at the very back of the hot little room, and stared at three terrible paintings above the licensing director's head, which showed mountains in golden romantic light and the same angler in each scene, landing a flopping trout while his wife and children beamed at him from the shore.

Before Raza could continue looking through his beat book, a man in a blue pastel suit, his shirt collar opened, walked in and went directly to the licensing director's desk. Darya Ali Raza pushed back his chair, shook hands, gave the man a hug, then chatted affably with him for several minutes while the Americans and their booking agent cooled their heels. The man in the pastel suit produced several hundred rupees and with an absolutely fluid gesture slipped the folded wad into Raza's large shirt pocket. Shortly thereafter, Raza returned to his desk, said "Excuse me" to the Americans, and filled out the licensing forms for the briber. When the man had left, he returned to his beat book, going down the columns, and sighing.

"Not a good one left," he said. "All taken, except the distant ones, of course."

The Americans, still unable to take his hint, sat silently as a bedraggled-looking messenger slunk through the door and laid a document by Raza's elbow. Continuing his charade at the beat book, the licensing director ignored the piece of paper. The messenger, however, gathered his courage and pushed the note a centimeter closer. It touched the director's arm and he started as if seeing it for the first time.

"Out!" he thundered.

The messenger scuttled to the veranda like a crab.

"Is it always like this?" said the Foreign Service wife to the booking agent.

"It is high season, you know," he replied.

The Foreign Service husband leaned toward the booking agent and whispered in his ear. The booking agent shut his eyes with relief and leaned across the desk, while his hand moved deftly from his pocket to the licensing director's hand.

"Ah," said Raza, sliding his hand from his desktop into his trouser pocket and back to the beat book where he pointed to the bottom of the page. "Right here." He beamed a lavish smile. "A fine beat indeed. Missed it completely."

The couple signed their forms. The booking agent paid the fees. They stood and left. Raza, the fan blowing his hair, turned to me and said, "May I help you?"

"Perhaps," said I, taking a deep breath. Then I told him that I wanted no well-known beat—not the Phalgam, Sind, or Lidder rivers. Nor did I want to stay in a lodge. Most of all, I didn't need a guide or gillie. All I wanted, I said, was to fish some high lakes in the northern Kashmir Himal, the most distant of distant beats.

"A fine choice," he said in a friendly tone, which made me wary. "Please fill out this form."

While I wrote in my passport number, Indian tourist visa number, place of issue, date of expiration, foreign and local addresses, father's surname and address, mother's name and address, and my intended date of departure from the subcontinent, as well as the lakes where I wanted to fish, another booking agent came in and sat down next to me. Raza ignored me until he finished chatting with him. Then he looked at the application that I had been holding out and said, "But what days do you want to fish each lake?"

"I don't know," I said. "Whenever I get there."

"This will never do," he said. "You must stipulate the day you will fish each beat, and if you put down two lakes for the same day, as you've done here and here, you must pay the appropriate licensing fee for each one. In other words, double price each day."

At this point, the booking agent, a sharp little man who needed a shave, said, "And you'll never get up to Gangabal that way. It's too steep."

"Really?"

"Yes," he said, adding, "With which group are you?"

"I'm alone."

"Do you know there are bears up there?"

"So I've heard."

"I suggest that you go with a group or cancel your plans," the booking agent said firmly, and Raza handed me back my application.

Right below my feet, on the first floor of the tourist complex, was the office of Indian Airlines. If there hadn't been a two-hour wait there, and if I hadn't known that getting out of Srinagar in the next week by air was virtually impossible, and that getting out overland was absolutely impossible because of the Sikh uprisings in the Punjab, I would have walked out the door and left for home without a backward glance. But sometimes you have only one move.

I took back my application, scratched out a lake on each of my "double" days, and handed it to Raza. Knight to queen's bishop 3. "The route stays," I said.

"As you wish," said Raza, beginning to scribble impatiently on the red licensing documents. He made out a copy for each lake, banged in the appropriate stamps, and handed them across the desk for my signature. I passed him several hundred rupees, and as I signed my name on the documents the booking agent said, "You should reconsider." Ignoring him, I folded the papers, placed them in my breast pocket, and walked out without reading them. This was an oversight.

At this point—to give you the full, frustrating details of wetting a line in the Himalaya—I might tell you how my friend Larry MacDonnell tried for two days to telephone Delhi so as to change his international flight and come trout fishing with me. Though he tried booking both an "urgent" call and a "lightning" connection, which costs twenty dollars for three minutes, he was unable to get through. And so my friend Paul Clark, who lives on the Thompson River in the Bitterroot Range of Montana, came instead. I might also tell you how our houseboat proprietor, Rasheed, a sincere and helpful man in his thirties, his teeth stained with nicotine and his hair gray from his two wives, tried to arrange a posh trek for us. Emptying his cigarette of tobacco and priming it with hashish, an act he contrived to do about eight times a day while lounging on the divan of his houseboat's porch, he said, "You can have a cook and a cookboy, wonderful curries and biriyanis every night, ponies to carry everything—even your cameras—tents, a guide, an assistant guide, and two horse handlers."

We had had a similar retinue on the mountain and wanted nothing so much as to get away from the grand excursion in the style of the old sahibs. But Rasheed, more used to tourists than mountaineers, couldn't understand our desire to rough it. And explaining what we enjoyed about hunting and fishing on our own in the Rockies was like explaining the act of love to a virgin.

"You have to do it, Rasheed," I said.

At the speed at which Raza had issued my fishing license, Paul and I negotiated with our kind and slothful houseboat owner, finally agreeing that he would do no more than hire us a taxi to the roadhead and procure us a brace of ponies.

"Remember," I said on the evening before we departed, "we need those horses."

"No problem," said Rasheed. "Trust me."

As we drove up the Sind Valley the next morning, having paid ten times the fare of the public bus, which took all day to make the two-hour taxi journey, I thought that if I caught only one eight-ounce trout on this, my third Himalayan trek, such a small amount of salmonid flesh would have cost approximately eighteen thousand dollars a pound and would have exacted enough energy that, had it been exerted in some place like Argentina or New Zealand, might have earned me a place in the record books. We all have our own grails.

We reached the village of Naranag, high in the pines by the clear and fast Wangat River. Rasheed, looking out of place in his gray town slacks and sandals, disappeared behind a gate while the taxi driver inspected his chassis. Paul and I waited. Ten minutes later, Rasheed appeared, a hashish cigarette smoking between his fingers. "There are no ponies," he said.

In India, one learns to take such news in stride. Resigned to our fate, Paul and I emptied our food bags of cabbages, carrots, and onions. We each left a parka and our extra underwear. I took out my second camera body and two long lenses. Still, I was not happy when I put on my pack. Paul, shouldering his, said, "Ugh."

"What did you say?" said Rasheed, extending his hand.

"Ugh."

"Do you have a gun?" he asked, shaking my hand.

"Why?"

"The bears."

"Bah," I said.

"What?" said Rasheed.

"Bah, humbug," I said distinctly.

"Be careful of the Gujars, too," he mentioned.

"The shepherds?" asked Paul.

"Bad men," said Rasheed, getting into the taxi. Sticking his head out the window, he added, "Leave nothing unattended. They'll steal it all. Have a good time." Spinning his tires, the taxi driver left in a billow of dust.

It was a four-thousand-foot climb and thirteen-mile hike to the first lake. The trail took us through a forest of long-needle pines, over a loamy trail scented with resin, and above the silver flumes of the vanishing Wangat River. It wound up toward parks of new green sedge rising toward broken gray mountains and glaciers. This was ibex country, the home of bharals and snow leopards, and because of one P. J. Mitchell, lt. col., ret., it had trout. White queen to black queen 8. Check.

There are places in every nation of the planet, places just beyond the last road, places that still lie within the jurisdiction of the men with their blue stamps and ledgers but that, in reality, belong to none of us and all of us. One only needs perseverance to get there. We climbed. And the packs hurt.

Not much to do about that. Going slow, we ascended through

cow parsnip, over fallen pinecones thick as your arm, and out of the swaying tall trees at what my altimeter called 10,800 feet. But I hadn't calibrated the instrument at a known elevation for days and so 10,800 was at best a good guess. Here, cows and horses grazed on long slopes of bright turf, and in the distance, where the trail undulated across two ridges, a man in a turban and a woman in a burgundy shawl led some goats. Forget-me-nots grew in pods, and yellow avens ran in fields toward a spring where miner's lettuce clung to the damp rocks. Above our water stop, from a pile of boulders, a marmot raised a shriek and leapt from sight.

We drank and then followed the trail across the ridge where the shepherds had disappeared, only to find another and another ridge stretching before us. The redstarts, tail feathers bursting like maroon kaleidoscopes, clipped neatly around us as we stopped and gazed at the route. We didn't pull out a map. It seemed pointless. One of the two we had, from a Japanese trekking book, showed the Himalaya from Pakistan to Nepal. Another, without contours or shaded relief, had the half dozen lakes for which we aimed placed beneath a stylized peak called Harmukh, which was about equidistant between the road we had left and the one we hoped to exit on. Trying to follow a route on these sheets was somewhat like trying to find a lake in the middle of Maine with a map that showed all of New England—a map that, it might be added, had been drawn by a German who had spoken to a Chinaman who had visited the area a half dozen years before with a guide who spoke only Urdu. We knew one thing, though: the lakes lay west.

We hiked; we stopped; we ate some of the brown bread we had bought in Srinagar. To the southwest, a glaciated peak had risen above the ridge system we traversed, and we assumed that this was Harmukh, and that where its glaciers fell—behind a dark emerald hogback, behind which the sun was also setting—we would find the lakes.

Back in the 1800s, this sort of hit-or-miss travel was common. In fact, in pursuit of the greatest unsolved problem of Asian geography—the location of the headwaters of the Indus, Sutlej, Ganga, and Tsangpo-Brahmaputra rivers—the Royal Geographic Society, the Indian Survey, and the British Army sent out numerous explorers, fakirs, and officers on lengthy missions from which some never returned. Sven Hedin, the Swedish explorer who spent a good part of his adult life in the Tibetan highlands, devoted himself to finding this navel of the world where the four great rivers met. On the way, not a few ibex, Marco Polo sheep, Tibetan antelope, and wild yaks were killed and eaten by these explorers, who thought nothing of living off the land for a couple of years. The most fascinating aspect of this exploration was that everyone involved was aware of its utter commercial uselessness. Unlike Magellan's circumnavigation, Columbus's crossing of the Atlantic, Lewis and Clark's march across the North American continent, or the winning of spheres of influence in Central Asia during the great game between Britain and Russia, the placing on the map of Mount Kailas, from whose four slopes the four sacred rivers of Asia flow, served no purpose other than to satisfy an eccentric geographic curiosity.

For me, to catch one trout that lived in the Himalaya, the abode of the snow, had become such a quest. And topography was not going to make the last bit easy. Losing the sunlight, we climbed along a streambed that roared between boulders. The tundra rose in steps before us. We surmounted what seemed to be a last flat ridge, which had a depression behind it. Here, we had to crane our heads back to see Harmuk's sharp summit. We met the sun again, and in its last light came over a rise and saw that the depression was occupied by a lake. A glacier and water-fall fell into its far end, another waterfall plunged from the ridge that formed the adjacent shore, while a broad clear stream left the bank on which we stood. The tarn was perhaps a mile across and on its calm surface lay the rings of feeding trout.

We walked along the shore and put down our packs on a flat spot. Paul climbed a nearby hill as I assembled my spinning rod. In a few minutes, I walked out on an archipelago of stones, made a long cast, turned the handle, and was fast to a trout. He made three darting runs, then came in splashing and cartwheeling. I picked him up, gave him a blow to the head, and laid him on the grass, the fruit of three circumnavigations of the globe, 350 miles of walking and ninety-three days of camping out. He was ten inches long.

A sudden medley of bleating made me look up. Several hundred sheep had surrounded our gear. They ate my map case, pulled apart Paul's clothes, nibbled our pads, and peered stupidly at the stove. I ran up to the flock, shouting and waving my arms while a Gujar shepherd boy in rags tittered and squealed at my antics. I waved a hand at him, and, still laughing, he began to toss rocks at his sheep. When we had cleared the campsite he sat on a rock and watched me catch another ten-incher, which I also kept. Then Paul took over the rod and released a dozen fish, all clones.

The sun had set. The Gujar boy had taken his sheep over the ridge. I sat on my pad, lit the stove, made some tea, and as Paul and I drank our evening brew, I dropped some butter into the skillet and began to fry the trout.

"May I see your fishing license?" asked a slim young man who had walked up to us in the dusk. He had a full head of black curly hair, a black mustache, and wore a khaki shirt and trousers. Except for his plastic sandals, he looked official.

"Are you a warden?" I asked.

"I am a warden."

I rummaged through my books and maps and produced the sheaf of papers.

The warden sat on the grass by our stove and studied the documents.

"This is July tenth," he said.

"I know."

"Your license . . ." He pointed to the documents. "The eleventh."

"No!" I exclaimed. "At the fisheries office I asked for the tenth." This was a lie. But who, coming upon a lake filled with rising trout after he has traveled for years to see the sight, would have resisted?

"No problem," he said good-naturedly, though it sounded like he wasn't quite sure if "no problem" was the correct English idiom. Then he studied the papers again and said, "This is not Gangabal Lake. Gangabal is up there." He pointed to the waterfall on the opposite shore.

"Oh, really."

"Yes. But no problem."

This was a warden after my own heart. He now looked down at my rod, lying on the grass.

"This is a spinning rod," he said.

"Yes. That is a spinning rod."

"Spinning rods are not allowed."

"Really?"

"Yes. It says on your license." He pointed to the back of the document, which I hadn't bothered to read. It read, in English almost as plain as day: "Use of spinning rods, spinners or spinning real [*sic*] is strictly prohibited."

This was a calamitous turn of events. I had been caught fishing on the wrong day in the wrong lake with the wrong tackle. Of course, I wanted to continue to fish tomorrow.

I had only one recourse—to use a variation of Rasheed's nonplussed defense, "There are no ponies." With a deadpan, Asian face, I said, "I didn't know."

"Only flies are allowed," he replied.

"I have only a spinning rod," I said.

He looked at the rod. He looked at the evidence, the two brown trout frying in the skillet. He looked at the poacher.

"What country?" he asked.

"America," I said.

"Where are you going?"

"Erin. Other side of range."

"You have only a spinning rod?"

"I have only a spinning rod."

"Sure?"

"Positive."

He looked at the fish again; at the rod; at me. "No problem," he said and handed me back my license.

White bishop to black queen 8. Mate.

"Want some trout?" I asked, proffering the skillet.

"Never eat fish," said the warden with a smile.

PORNO TROUT

As a kid, I had wildlife pornography all over my bedroom walls. There was the painting of the white-tailed buck, neck swelled, antlers dusted with snow, poised behind a broken fence on a November evening filled with storm. There was the cougar, lying on the branch of a pine tree as he stared across an alpine basin dense with conifers. And there was the elk, bugling in a golden meadow before the glaciers of Mount Moran in northwestern Wyoming.

Best of all there was the trout, sleek and curving from the water, arcing toward a fly whose leader had been tangled around a jutting branch so the fly, a dry fly, hung a foot above the current. In the background, in the muted greens and browns that used to adorn the cover of the L. L. Bean catalog, was the small and astonished form of the hapless angler.

This trout, a great female trout, whose flanks mixed most of the iridescent colors of a rainbow and most of the opalescent colors of a river's stones, was the sexiest of my wildlife porn because even as a kid full of heady dreams I knew that she was unattainable. I could shoot deer and elk, I could catch bass left, right, and center, I could knock a goose out of the sky at forty-five yards, but I simply did not have the trout gene—I could not cast a fly line very well, I could not tie good knots in my tapered leaders, I could not mend my line gracefully; worst of all, I could not think like a trout, I could not even catch trout when the stocking truck dumped them in the stream at my feet and six-year-olds, with dime-store plastic reels and misaligned rods and who had never even seen a dry fly, slipped in front of me and caught two-pound rainbows using cat food.

When it came to fishing for wild trout I felt even more humiliated. I was always too late or too early for the hatch; the water was too hot or too cold; if the trout were feeding on number 22 midges I would only have 18s; if I actually hooked a trout, my hook would be embedded in the top of its head, or in its flank, or in its gill, meaning that maybe the fish hadn't wanted my fly at all and had turned away at the last instant, not fooled by my clumsy presentation. In the sporting world, where the dry-fly fisherman sits at the very pinnacle of achievement, I was a failure, the wimp on the beach blanket, sand kicked in his face as the lifeguard walked away with the girl in the bikini.

Reminding myself (as I did constantly) that I was a good angler for other species and a really good hunter and that I even caught trout, big trout, on spinning lures did little good. It was like saying I was a genius at calculus but hopeless around girls. Trout on flies, on *dry* flies, was where it was at for everyone I respected. It was the ultimate form of fishing. It was erotic.

So I become a good faker. I bought all the right gear: neoprene waders, a graphite rod, and fancy fishing vest not bulged with too many fly boxes, showing that I knew what I really needed and wasn't carrying around a bunch of extra junk. I could even name, in Latin, the insect life that crawled under and flew over rivers. I became a decent caster and caught some average trout, mostly nymphing, which is a sturdy and sensitive form of fly-fishing but never wins the oohs and ahs of the angling world the way dry fly-fishing does. And a couple of times, when I really paid attention and just spent some days with a river and myself and the fish, I actually caught some lovely trout, trout that made me feel good to the marrow of my bones. But I never caught the porno trout, a centerfold fish like the one on my boyhood calendar.

So I paid.

I paid money to guides, which, if you rate the various form of fish prostitution, is the cleanest. And alongside of these men (and a few women) I caught gi-normous fish on tiny flies and light tippets, the kind of fish that if they were human females you'd say, "Breast implants."

And I paid in that other kind of way, which is not so clean, tagging along with my friends who truly had the trout gene, going to their spots, watching what flies they cast, copying *exactly* what they did, and every once in a while catching a gi-normous trout—all of which reminded me of being a traveler in some exotic land and befriending the sultan, who would say, "You've been looking kind of lonely, old buddy. Why not take Princess Number 27 to bed with you tonight?" And leading her away, she'd look at me with these eyes (the trout's giving a quick flip of its tail as I released it), which said, "You couldn't catch me by yourself if you worked at it for ten million years."

This is what comes from a misspent youth, idled away over trout magazines. This is what happens when you keep the Trout Unlimited calendar under your mattress.

So I paid, and I copied, and I caught rainbows in Wyoming, and cutbows in Colorado, and char in Alaska, and browns in New Zealand—these six-pound trout, these nine-pound trout, these eighteen-pound salmon, wondering if I was becoming like those guys who take sex holidays to Bangkok, who know about forty-six different ways to do it, but have never had a real date in their life.

It was ironic, then, that while on a sex holiday in New Zealand, I had my chance. I had gotten totally burned out crawling up rivers behind guides who wore khaki shirts and floppy bush hats, who tied flies on the end of my line faster than I could have thought about it, and who whispered "Cast there now!" as if my life and the future of humanity depended on my making the cast. And when I caught these trout, they said no more than "Grand fish," in another stage whisper, as they slipped these incredible trout back into the water, trout that if you had caught them back home in an earlier time, you would have drug their tails around town for an entire day, hanging them on scales in the tackle shop, the hardware store, and the butcher's while having your picture taken with other anglers and the mayor. The state newspaper would have gone so far as to send down a photographer, putting your photo on the front page right underneath a plane crash that killed 131 people.

And after the guides and I had gone up and down these streams as if we were playing Monopoly, and I caught fish like clockwork morning and evening, I started getting the feeling that maybe these fellows had caught these trout about a dozen times apiece, while they and I (of course) exclaimed, "Oh, my God, wow, amazing," at just the right times, the way they do in Bangkok and all the world over.

Which is when I decided to go fishing by myself, walking up the rivers of Kiwi Land and walking back down the same rivers, seeing them in reverse, and occasionally catching these teeny trout while meeting almost no other anglers. Two or three times a giant trout, looking more like a barracuda than a freshwater fish, came up to my fly from some deep cerulean pool only to look at my fly and sink back into the depths like a dream.

I walked and I walked, and I cast and I cast, liking the tawny light and the silence even more, and how the rod felt in my hand while the line rolled out on a windless morning, enjoying how the river tugged at my feet as I thought about quests—a big trout, a demanding mountain, a soulful woman (not always in that order)—and the tension created when patience finally meets desire. And I reckoned how someday, if I worked at it long enough, I might describe the dense webs of life in which I was caught, describe them with rapture and wonder, and without the ego I knew that I still needed to lose.

It was there, wading those rivers, that I understood what I had known before in South America but had lost: fishing, at least river fishing, had never really meant catching trout for me, which is probably why I hadn't been very good at that task most of the time. Instead, trout were the reason for the rod, which was the implement that kept me from looking foolish as I conducted words into the melody of water . . . into the air of the world . . . painting with fly line all the colors of the sentences that I would someday write. Rivers were my pen and scratch pad and far better than a desk to transubstantiate what the world was singing.

So in the pregnancy of returning to this understanding, I was walking up a river, a river that I won't name because about seven thousand anglers would be there within a year if I did. And walking up this river I did think, once again, that it would be nice, at least once, to find a spot that no one else had pointed out to me, that I was led to by my unconscious feet, that had no presuppositions attached to it, that when I saw it I would be startled into the recognition of our connection, and there, actually there, I would catch a trout that not only matched my fantasies but which I also felt good about.

And then—I guess because it started to rain—I forgot about catching this fish and just enjoyed that strange and lovely landscape, full of low clouds and dank smells, a landscape that smells like no other place in the world, as if Antarctica got mixed up with a rain forest while trying to impersonate the Rocky Mountains, lonely, private, and spacious all at once, and also underlaid by a tender embrace, which, at least for me, is the best feeling to have about a country because you feel that the country cares about you.

Feeling this way, as if the country had my heart in its hand and was holding it, I looked at the river, rushing by me gray and overhung by clouds. Far ahead was a gorge, the river parting around a boulder train and forming two parallel rapids. These two rapids met below the boulders and flowed into a widening of the stream, which became riffled opposite me and quiet a bit farther on, the river bouncing along with a tannic glow. There, on the far bank, a fallen tree stretched partly into the river, its topmost branch like a black and bony finger pointing down into the current.

I thought, *Now, that would be a good spot for a fish,* and I hiked on, looking forward to drying my gear in the hut that lay a couple of miles ahead. There, I ate my dinner on the covered porch and drank a cup of tea as the rain stopped and the clouds partially lifted. Thinking about the fallen tree and the trout that I had understood to lie beneath it, I assembled my rod, took a box of flies, and hiked downstream, casting first in the gorge as a way of understanding this stretch of the river before actually coming to the spot where I wanted to fish.

The evening was damp and cool and gray, losing its light, when I finally came to the spot where the finger pointed into the current. I took off my New Zealand dry fly, which had come well recommended, and tied on a red-and-white dry fly, which I knew from home and upon which I had caught some fish. I sent a cast upstream from the fallen tree. The fly floated under the black branch and on downstream. I lifted the line, cast again, and mended. When the fly floated under the tree a second time, the river fell away beneath it. In the place where the river had been, a red fish swirled. Then a trout jumped higher than the fallen tree, about three feet above the surface of the water, and it was two feet long, looking the way trout are supposed to look on calendars except that it was upside-down and was a male, the red-and-white fly embedded in the corner of his enormous hooked jaw.

When he hit the water he was instantly downstream, all my fly line was gone, and the backing made a huge arc against the current as I ran after him. No sooner had I reached him, retrieving my line as I ran, than he shot upstream, most of the line going out again. I sprinted up the bank just as he turned and headed the other way. For about ten seconds I felt nothing on the end of the line as I frantically reeled, and then he was there, solid and much closer.

I had no net and no waders, so I simply walked into the river and tried to lead him to shore. But he would have none of it and ran back across the river. He made three more runs before I was able to slide him onto the stones. I had no scale, no tape measure either, so I just looked at him, lying on the small and glistening rocks. He was about half the size of the big New Zealand trout I had caught with my guides, meaning in the language of pounds about four, but stunningly perfect in the way one's partner in deep romance always is. I unhooked him and slid him back into the river. Then, feeling electric, like the world was bathed in the buzz of heat lightning, I walked back to the hut, not meeting another angler and not knowing what I would have said had I met one. After twenty years of fly-fishing, how do you say, "I finally caught a trout."

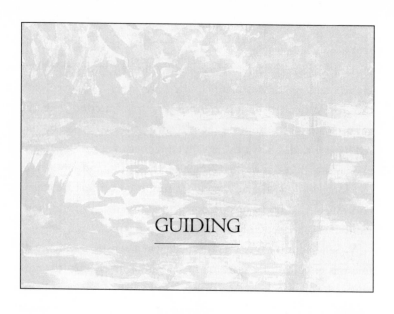

GUIDING

Sometimes when the phone rings you *know* that you shouldn't pick it up . . . that you should just let the answering machine handle it, with its volume turned way down, and that you should listen to the message maybe next year. But there's your hand on the receiver, and there's the voice of the trip leader you contacted last week, saying, "Well, you can have a free ticket because of our group-booking situation, and if you were willing to sort of be a guide once in a while, nothing much, just be a resource person once in a while, give the folks a few pointers about casting, matching the hatch, and also, *rrrummp* [massive throat clearing], if you could come through with that article you mentioned. . . ."

You know those air horns that go off when a submarine is about to dive—*aaraang, aaraang, aaraang?* That's what you should be hearing when someone says words like "free," "resource," and "article" in return for anything as chancy as fishing.

But you don't, not when the destination is a place like Bhutan, with its big snow mountains at the eastern end of the Himalaya that look like Shangri-La, and its jungles full of rare primates like golden langurs, and not-often-seen birds like giant hornbills, and tigers and elephants thrown in for good measure, and (you won't believe this but it's true) trout in the highlands, brought in, once again, by those indefatigable Brits, who saw a river anyplace in the world and said, "It simply must have trout." And because Bhutan is a Buddhist country and no one kills anything, or at least not until they're real hungry, the trout are huge. Given all that, you begin to rationalize: How bad can it be, talking to some other anglers for a week? It's only one more time; and how else can you get to Bhutan without paying for it?

So off I went to this faraway kingdom, one of a handful strung along the summits of the Himalaya, each providing the traveler with its own version of a koan: a Buddhist paradox whose answer comes through sudden enlightenment, sometimes pain, and never good common sense. Bhutan, the most insular and xenophobic of these kingdoms, didn't have a direct flight to it from anywhere in the world other than Calcutta or Dhaka, and pretty predictably, no one in either of these capitals or in Bhutan had thought of coordinating the flights up to Bhutan with the incoming overseas flights, so groups like ours were forced to spend two days "in transit" in one or the other of these cities. The trip leader chose Dhaka. I would have chosen Calcutta (the architecture is better), but people who have scammed a free ticket rarely get to offer their input on such matters.

We got off the jet on one of those premonsoon nights of southern Asia when, if you live in the temperate part of the globe, you think that the captain has made a mistake, landing in a sauna instead of a country. And we walked down onto the tarmac, because they don't have jetways in that part of the world, and into the doors of the terminal, which of course wasn't air-conditioned, and stood in line for about an hour while soldiers in green berets stamped people's passports.

When I got to the desk, the soldier said, "Passport. Visa." I was already handing him both. He had a huge black mustache, black eyes, and a bright white smile.

"You are a writer?" he said.

"I am a writer," I said, pleased that he had noticed.

"Tch-tch," he said and waved his hand across the room in the way that Asian men call a waiter.

Two guards with rifles appeared from the corners and grabbed me by the elbows.

"Take him upstairs," said the immigration officer.

After twenty-five years of traveling around the world and having been arrested nearly everywhere, I'm still astonished when it happens.

"Me? You can't mean *me.*"

They did.

We walked up an open staircase, the people on our fishing trip looking on with their fly-rod cases in their hands and their mouths hanging open. At an office at the top of the stairs, its glass door frosted, one guard knocked, waited until an authoritarian voice barked, and they led me in.

A colonel-like person sat at a desk and spoke into a phone. I was seated on a chair against the wall, to the side of his desk, and the guards left. The colonel-like person ignored me for about five minutes, talking away in what was gibberish to me. So I ignored him as well, taking out the magazines that I had learned to carry on these trips, which show that I am a bona fide natural history and fishing writer.

After about twenty minutes, when it was obvious to the officer that I wasn't sweating (I sure wasn't going to show him that I was nervous), he hung up, looked at my papers, and said, "We don't like writers in Bangladesh."

"I'm sorry," I said. "I'm just a fishing writer and I'm going to

Bhutan. We're only staying in Dhaka because our connecting flight doesn't leave until the day after tomorrow."

"We don't like writers," he repeated. "They cause trouble."

"I'm just a fishing writer," I said again, in case he hadn't heard me, and placed the magazines, open to my stories, on his desk.

He leafed through them.

"Didn't you know that we don't want writers in Bangladesh?"

"I had heard something like that. But I thought it better to be honest on my visa application."

Looking at a photograph of a tiger that I had taken in India, he said, "Do you know that we have the largest tiger reserve in the world?"

"I do. The Sunderbans."

"Why didn't you visit them?"

"It was easier to get a visa to India."

Ah, honesty. It never gets you anyplace in the Third World, maybe not even in the First. Pissed off that I had spurned his Sunderbans, he closed the magazines, shoved them at me, plucked a large stamp from the top of his desk, and slammed it onto my visa and passport.

"One-day transit visa," he said.

"But our connecting flight leaves the day after tomorrow."

"That's your problem," he said, pushing my papers across his desk and dismissing me.

Out past the customs agents where the group had assembled with our luggage, I told my story to the bona fide trip leader and our huddled group. The leader, a tall, out-of-shape man in a pink shirt, khaki pants, and boating shoes, sighed. "We'll deal with it tomorrow," he said.

We did, driving around for three hours from green government building to green government building while the thermometer sat at a 105°F and the humidity at 99, which doesn't make you think of trout. It makes you think of gin and tonics. The air conditioner of the minivan labored fiercely and not quite effectively, and the group got bored and sultry despite the peppy talk of our tour guide, a plump lady in a blue sari who chatted on about mosques and gardens, which we were passing. As the group was left off at another historic site, she, the bona fide trip leader, and I would dash into a government office and trot down long corridors with lazy fans circling overhead. In angry, machine-gun language, our tour guide would accost small men, leaning over enormous desks filled with stacks of documents; the small men waved their arms ineffectually and sent us on.

At about noon, a client insurrection brewing and muttered undertones coming from the back of the bus—"Mmmzzzzza-aaa, mmmzzzzzaaa, mmmzzzzzaaaa"—we walked through the palm trees surrounding yet another green government building, up an outside staircase, and into a screened corner office where a middle-aged woman in a purple sari sat. Her desk faced a garden, and she looked important.

She heard our story, related by our tour guide in far more deferential tones than she had used with the male officials; she looked at the trip leader, his pink shirt drenched with sweat; and she listened again as the tour guide described how many trips the trip leader had brought through Dhaka, that his groups always stayed at the Hilton, and that I was writing for a big American magazine. She handed her a copy, open to a story about New Zealand. She pointed out the travel-arrangements section and repeated the word "advertising."

The woman, who looked like Indira Gandhi and who seemed to have heard every story every traveler had ever told and some that they hadn't, looked at my documents, looked at me—

running shoes, baggy pants, a white shirt that I had bought in a Kathmandu market—and sighed. I don't think that her sigh was so much about my appearance but about a world in which people were wasting her time to go trout fishing in another country while half her nation starved.

Taking a very small stamp from her sampler on a file cabinet, she made neat imprints on my passport and visa, signing within the boxes.

"You have a day extension," she said.

"Thank you," I said sincerely.

"May I take the liberty of suggesting that upon returning through Bangladesh you change your profession?"

I looked at her, surprised.

"Perhaps a fishing guide would be appropriate," she said, pulling at her chin.

I nodded in complete understanding.

The trip leader wrung her hand, almost weeping with relief. We ran down the stairs and went directly to the most expensive air-conditioned restaurant in the city, which of course was in the hotel where we were staying, the Hilton. For the next day and a half, no one moved from their rooms, the restaurant, the bar, and the pool. It was almost too hot to do anything except drink gin and tonics and occasionally turn the pages of a novel.

Naturally, after this not atypical greeting to southern Asia, all of us were hoping to find a friendly Himalayan respite—perhaps some blue skies over snowy mountains, crisp temperatures, the sort of subalpine weather that makes you feel absolutely tiptop, and sweet, smiling Buddhist monks pouring us tea.

But the only thing that was pouring in Bhutan was the rain, the clouds so low over the mountains that our plane nearly crashed into one as we approached the runway, the rock walls appearing so close to our port wingtip that I knew the pilot had made a serious error and that we had escaped death by simple good fortune. *And all this*, I thought, *for a goddamn fish.*

As the small plane bounced on the runway, I was totally rattled, my palms sweating, every ounce of color drained from my face, my heart in my throat. The trip leader, in the seat in front of me, leaned over and lost his breakfast in the air-sickness bag. We were the only two who had seen the near disaster. He turned around and put a finger to his deathly pale lips.

A Buddhist monk or two, offering solace, or at least steepling their palms and saying *tashi delay* (I salute the godhead within you), would have been welcome. But there were none at the airport, only bustling Bhutanese customs officials, tour guides, and assistant tour guides, and assistants to the assistants, all in maroon robes, efficient as Swiss burghers, moving us along through more forms, into the van, over to the capital, and into our rooms.

The rooms were cold, cold as those of a Scottish castle, after which the lodge was styled. We were served a poor lunch, saw an indigenous dance performed upon the lawn of the lodge, and were then driven to the river that flowed through the capital. When you have flown halfway around the world, spent four days traveling, and given up all the important things you do at home to catch a mythical trout in a poetry-filled land and instead catch a plastic bag out of what looks like an irrigation ditch in spate, you either get angry or remember that the reason you like being in Buddhist lands is that their ironies are always right on the surface. Some of the paying clients got angry.

"Tomorrow," the trip leader promised, "we'll be out in the country."

We were, and the country was filled with mud. The minivan, which didn't have four-wheel drive, got stuck every time we left the pavement, and the trip leader, our Bhutanese tour guide, his assistant, the assistant's assistant, and I got out and put our shoulders to the back of the van—heave-ho, lads, one, two, three, *zzzzzzz* went the tires—as the paying customers watched and said things like "Perhaps we should put some branches under the wheels." Or from the more jolly ones, "Do they have a Bhutanese A.A.A.?" while we got covered from head to foot with mud.

Wiping his face, the head tour guide, a short jolly man in maroon robes, said, "Very very very very very bad weather. Perhaps you come back next year." His assistant, a silent teenager, just smiled. The assistant to the assistant walked into the woods, and we never saw him again.

As we reboarded the van, the Commodore, an investment banker from Vancouver who had an upper-crust, British accent, said, "Well done," then "Expect the unexpected." Tall, handsome, his blond hair graying at the temples, he had become the immediate spokesman of the group. He wasn't a true, bona fide retired naval officer, but he did own a refitted frigate that he sent around the world ahead of him. He would then fly to the nearest airport to meet it and be picked up by his personal helicopter.

From his frigate, helicopter, and the several small fishing boats berthed on the larger craft, he fished about four months of every year. He had fished everywhere, and as we now drove to the next hot spot, he said, from his seat behind the driver, "Bla-bla-bla-bla-bla [place name], bla-bla-bla [species of fish], first-class! Haw-haw-haw-haw, eh?" The Bhutanese had refused his helicopter landing privileges and, "unfortunately," as he had said, he was on our trip.

Most of the Commodore's adventures had taken place with Gilbert (said Geebert), a Quebeçois commodities trader who was the Commodore's best friend and who had come along. A technophile, he had brought a dozen reel-and-line combinations and had employed a fly shop for well over a week tying four thousand flies for the trip, *all* of which he showed the trip leader and me, so that we knew that the number four thousand and the dozen reel-and-line combinations weren't hyperbole. He wanted to know if he had brought "the right stuff."

I said that with his tackle he could go anywhere in the world and feel secure.

To which he replied, "Monsieur, do not make fun of me. We amateurs need more equipment than you experts."

Incredibly thin, with an enormous hooked nose and sunken cheeks, Gilbert had also undergone recent triple-bypass surgery and the even more recent removal of portions of his stomach and intestinal tract because of cancer. At our first dinner, he showed us how they had done his two operations by arranging the left-over noodles on the serving platter. "Yes, they cut this artery and put in the new Teflon one right there. The stomach," he sidled over an eggplant with a serving spoon, shaving off its lower half, "they took one third."

I had thought, *Well, everyone has their story.* But on the next night, Gilbert rearranged the noodles once again, showing us what *would* happen to him if he needed another bypass, and if they had to take the rest of his intestines.

Suffice it to say that Gilbert's end of the table remained the medical corner. There, too, sat Lonnie and Lou Anne. Both were dressed in the standard Orvis catalog khaki, she brittle, blond, pretty, fortysomething, and addicted to Retin-A, so she had a perennially red face. Lonnie was huge, hands like boxing gloves, head like a red fire hydrant, and with a booming voice. The only reason that he let the Commodore speak so much was that he and Lou Anne were from south Texas, where they ran an exotic game ranch, and he felt intimidated by the Commodore's British accent.

Lonnie, quite naturally, was not intimidated by me. At our first meeting in the lobby of the Dhaka Hilton, he had crushed my hand in one of those outdoor-guy handshake duels: ho-ho, ha-ha, I'm just as big a he-man as you. "Been reading your stuff for years," he crowed.

After we let go of each other, he looked down at me. Even in my cowboy boots, which I hadn't brought along, I would have barely reached his chin. "But I always thought," he added, "by how you wrote, that you were a much bigger man."

Fortunately, there were three fairly—how can one say it—less colorful clients on the trip. One was Jean, the Commodore's fourth wife, a quiet person with dark red hair and beautiful elbows. She kept the sleeves of her khaki bush shirt rolled up and wore turquoise wool vests that matched her eyes. Holding a drink and listening to the Commodore go on and on, she would keep her elbows quite close to her sides, very relaxed, and her elbows seemed to say, "I have made my deal with the devil, and it is okay."

The second fairly sane person was TCR, which wasn't his name but the name of his ranch, the Tri County Ranch, which spanned three counties in New Mexico and was the size of half of Delaware, as he liked to say. TCR had white muttonchops, a liver-colored nose, a big belly, and wore lots of silver, as well as actual cowboy boots. He had brought several cases of red wine along with him because, as he mentioned, "Buying wine in Asia is like buying water in New Mexico. You can get it, but you're gonna pay." Looking at the cases of wine, I said that at least if the fishing were bad we'd have something to do.

"*Vaquero*," he said, slapping me on the back, "you know the lay of the land."

This may or may not have been true. The only lay of the land I presently wanted to know was Charlotte, the Commodore's daughter by his second wife. She was a sweet peach of a young woman, with the sort of unkempt curly brown hair that is supposed to make its wearer look like a forest nymph and, in this case, was very successful. She had savanna-colored eyes and a blush spot on each cheek and was a dead out, hopelessly bad angler. As she said, "I fish the way Victorian women used to have sex. I close my eyes and think of the flag."

The Commodore, after years of neglecting Charlotte, had decided to take an interest in her. "It was Jean," Charlotte explained. "She said that if he didn't start being a father to me, she'd stop sleeping with him. Sex. It's all connected to sex."

The Commodore had sent Charlotte to the Orvis Fishing School, where, according to her, she had graduated last in her class. "It's just not sexy," she chortled. "All of us dressed in neoprene suits, standing in the water, waving flyswatters in the air." She looked at me. "Wouldn't you rather be lying on the beach with no clothes on, reading a book?"

"Absolutely," I said. She smiled at me, flirting again, and made a weak cast. The tip of her rod, which she had obviously not seated firmly on the butt section, flew across the river, broke off her fly, and fell into the water, where it was swept away.

"Oops," said Charlotte.

I didn't know what to do: howl or dive into the river. She was casting a boron fly rod, which cost about nine hundred dollars.

"Don't worry," she said. "I have another one in the van. Actually two. I'm very careless."

Not a day later, she proved it. Closing the van's door on her rod and snapping it in two, she turned to me and said, "See, care-less."

She could have broken a boron fly rod every day for the next fifty years, and I wouldn't have cared. I think, really, that Charlotte and I would have fallen deeply goo-goo-eyed over each other had it not been for one impediment that came between us: My ex-girlfriend from New Zealand had come along.

Now, this disastrous mix-up happened as most uncomfortable situations happen: by not being honest with yourself and with others. Evelyn had phoned in the middle of the night, and we had had one of those echoey, satellite-transmitted talks.

"I miss you," she said.

"Well . . . I miss you too."

"I want to do something with you."

"Well . . ."

"Are you coming over to fish this summer?"

Evelyn was an amazingly fine angler. Both her father and mother had been on the New Zealand national team.

"Not exactly," I said. "Actually I'm going to Bhutan."

Bright idea, I had thought: way too expensive for her.

"Who's running the trip?"

I gave her the number.

And just like that she booked it. Just like that.

I had forgotten that attorneys—even New Zealand ones—can afford anything.

So there was Evelyn, with her long, frizzy, strawberry-blond hair and steady blue eyes, who could fish the pants off any man. And there was Charlotte, who reminded me of savannas and who I wished would fish the pants off me.

And after dinner on the third night—the fishing execrable be-cause of the rain, and everyone, especially the trip leader, drinking too much because of it—Evelyn and I went to our room and found ourselves in the same bed, even though we had agreed— had even shook hands—on being "just friends." Maybe it was all of TCR's red wine, but there we were, making all the right noises without having any of the right feelings to go along with the sound effects. Afterward, as we lay in the dark, she turned to me and said, "So you really didn't want me to come."

"I always want you to come."

"Be serious. To Bhutan."

She was angry, but so was I. "When you phoned me," I said, "had you broken up with someone?" I couldn't understand why she had wanted to start all this again when we had called it quits at least twice before.

"I had just broken up with someone," she said grudgingly. "Did I make you feel guilty when I called?" she asked, her voice lightening.

"You made me feel guilty," I said.

I looked at her lovely peaches-and-cream face in the dark and put my arms around her.

"It's a shame," I said, "that two people who know each other so well are always a hairbreadth from getting it together."

"It's you," she said, smiling her cool prosecutor's smile.

"Me?"

"You can never really like a redhead."

"Come on."

"We're not gullible women." She gave me a little kiss. "And you can't scam us."

This was only partially true. The truth was I had never been able to scam her, so I said nothing.

She sighed and said, "It's only one more week. And if you so much as give Charlotte one more come-hither look I will slit your throat in your sleep." She kissed me again, so sweetly, and snuggled against my chest.

Under this felicitous arrangement, we completed the trip. The fishing continued to be awful, pounding rain falling daily, the rivers flooded torrents. We couldn't even get to the streams that were reputed to have the really large trout because all the secondary roads were washed out.

To make matters worse, when we asked our Bhutanese guides if we could walk up the secondary roads, they exchanged nervous looks, as if maybe they had a stash of weapons-grade plutonium cached up there, and said, "Oh, good fishing very very very very very far. Too far to walk. Maybe next year."

If we insisted, they stood in the road and said, "Not possible. We must go now." And like goats, we were shepherded back to the van.

In addition, the Bhutanese cuisine was heavy and greasy, even by Himalayan standards, which doesn't stint on the oil and which made everyone feel slightly queasy. With no fishing stories from the day to divert them and with a sort of general malaise in the gut, people found Gilbert just the right depressing antidote to the depressing situation.

He had run out of locations into which his cancer might metastasize and had begun diagramming his wife's diabetes and its attendant complications. At the other end of the table, the Commodore's voice, ever upbeat, went on, "Bla-bla-bla, bla-bla-bla, haw-haw-haw, eh?" He became intolerable even to the trip leader, who could tolerate anything, and who, I became convinced, had been a prisoner in the Gulag before graduating to an adventure-travel fishing guide.

Before the trip broke into internecine client backbiting, he pulled out the trip leader's final solution: me. Just as the Commodore went into his "When I was in Patagonia" routine, and Gilbert had begun to demonstrate how they had amputated his wife's legs, the trip leader turned to me and said, "Haven't you fished near there in Patagonia?" This, of course, was my cue to hold up my end of the bargain for my all-expenses-paid, once-in-a-lifetime fishing trip to the other side of the world.

Folding my napkin, I said, "Well, yes. This is many years ago, of course . . ."

And the Commodore leaned back in his chair, looking almost relieved as he nipped the end of his cigar with a golden cutter. And Gilbert put aside his serving-spoon scalpels, and TCR refilled his wineglass.

Charlotte, sweet Charlotte, was already gone from the table, reading in a corner, and Evelyn was watching me with those eyes that said, "You are a scumbag but I love you," which made me feel fairly guilty, as well as a fool for throwing her away. But I was onstage, and people were waiting. On and on I prattled, pulling out the old commodores from the past trips, with their funny accents and eccentricities (of course not calling them commodores), and all the old crackers, except since Lonnie and Lou Anne were from the South I made them the New England Brahmins with their tight Yankee sphincters, which made Lonnie and Lou Anne guffaw, and I ended up with the real guides outfishing me, and the Argentine customs agent mistaking my can of Mace for underarm deodorant and spraying it mockingly under his armpit, which emptied the entire customs outpost in a stampede of coughing tourists and weeping soldiers and which landed me in jail overnight.

When the laughter had stopped, Evelyn said, "He actually caught some big sea-run browns in Tierra del Fuego." That is where we had met.

"If I did," I said, "it was because she stopped catching them long enough to show me how." And for a few seconds it was as if everyone in the room had quit whipping the conversational waters with false casts and just made a neat, no-nonsense toss, pretty, crisp, and essential.

"She's a great angler," I said. "The best."

"Hear, hear," said TCR, raising his glass. "To the women."

We raised our glasses.

The next day, Jean, no flashy angler but steady and knowledgeable, caught the only large fish of the trip, a two-foot-long brown trout on a streamer. The fish must have been wearing night-vision glasses to have seen her fly in the muddy river, and she played it expertly, releasing it quickly, under no one's eyes except TCR's and mine. Standing up, she said, "Well, the Commodore will have to eat that one."

Unfortunately, he didn't. Her story went untold at our planned last-night celebratory dinner because the van got stuck again in the mud, and as we pushed it out the transmission broke. By the time a rescue van could come, it was 10 P.M., and we didn't get back to the capital until four in the morning, which left us little time to pack before our 6 A.M. departure.

Dozing on the plane, dead tired, spattered with mud, Evelyn sleeping next to me and Charlotte's head nodding down the aisle, I looked at the flooded fields of Bangladesh beneath us and thought, *Well, at least I'm not down there.*

But then reality set in: *I caught a few ten-inch trout and spent a significant amount of my time and other people's money doing it. I got no story, or at least nothing that anyone will ever publish, plus the photos are wretched. And I have a scratchy urethra because Evelyn caught chlamydia from her last boyfriend, thought she got rid of it, but didn't. Bummer. And no antibiotics till the States. This is it! No more guiding. No more faking it.* We walked into the immigration hall of the Dhaka International Airport, sorted ourselves into queues, and even from a hundred feet away I could see our line proceeding toward the very immigration agent who had checked us in last time.

Bad karma, I thought, reaching into my small carry-on.

A few minutes later, I handed him my visa and passport. He looked up, his deep black eyes locking onto mine in startled recognition. It hadn't been a week since he had checked me through. His grin turned wolfish, and he pointed at me, saying, "Writer."

Cool as the air-conditioned Hilton bar, where I hoped that I would soon be drinking, I pointed to my visa and said, "Fishing guide."

Disconcerted, he looked down at the document that I had changed a minute before. If possible his grin became even more predatory, changing however from pleasure at my misfortune to appreciation. He plucked up his stamp, struck it magisterially on the papers, and dashed off his signature.

Handing me my documents, he boomed, "Welcome, fishing guide, to Bangladesh!"

Ever after, I have considered it one of my more enlightened entries into Asia.

THE LEWIS in the FALL

In the Rockies, in the fall, at least for a short time, it's possible to suspend your disbelief. The fine mild weather, the golden mountainsides, the sense that you are young in a youthful and precious moment, let you ignore the knowledge that snow is a few weeks—or just a night—away. The still-unsullied beauty of most of the countryside lets you think that most people will feel as you do about it and leave it alone. Driving home from my tour of the proposed New World Mine, on the border of Yellowstone National Park, it remained hard for me to believe that half a billion dollars of gold and silver could really convince people to risk a deluge of toxic tailings down one of the most stunning canyons of the planet—the Clark Fork of the Yellowstone—and endless ore trucks and power lines through grizzly country.

I had put a rod and waders in the car along with my camping gear, somehow knowing that when the tour of the mine was done, I'd be unhappy and would want to stop and fish on my way home across Yellowstone. Casting in moving water, whether surf or river, has always been meditation for me—a going down to find peace and to let go.

Passing all of my old favorite places on the Yellowstone and Firehole rivers, which now had many cars at their trailheads, I drove along the Lewis River in the southern part of Yellowstone Park, not stopping at the famous meadow where everyone has to fish because it looks like a postcard of how trout fishing in the Rockies is supposed to look: golden grass, the hills in the middle distance covered with pines, the far mountains covered with snow. Instead, I parked at the rim of the canyon slightly farther on, where no one fishes because you just about have to rock-climb down to the water.

Such strategies—searching out gnarly access routes and setting off during storms—ensure privacy in country that only twenty years ago was a great cache of private and solitary mountains. In fact, as recently as the late 1970s I walked through valleys that had waist-high flowers and no evidence of other humans having been there within a hundred years, not even a trail. Then came environmental awareness followed by environmental appetite. The cost of having extolled the enjoyment of wild places has been that the mountains are now full of hikers, boaters, climbers, mountain bikers, skiers, paragliders, wildlife photographers, anglers, and hunters. We now have a constituency to protect wild places, but each of us has to become more enterprising to find a smidgen of quiet and meditative space.

Which is why Merle, my golden Lab, and I were creeping down the crumbling sandstone, using the lodgepole pines as belay stations and the downsloping, rotten ledges as connective avenues between barely negotiable drops. As we slid over the last cliff and to the river's side, our removal from the upper world was complete. The road could not be seen, the sound of moving water filled the air. It was mid-afternoon and the sunlight slanted into the canyon. A breeze blew downstream, the golden halos of aspen trembling. The willows, green and burgundy tinged, hemmed the turquoise water, which sprayed haze against the black rock.

I rigged the rod; Merle had a drink; we walked upstream.

It had been a year of drought, following many years of drought, and in places the river flowed as no more than a narrow, luminescent channel between the tabular rocks of the riverbed. The hydrological conditions—almost no river—made finding the fish easy.

Stripping line from the reel, I sent a cast upstream, but the line slid back down the guides and collapsed at my feet. I hadn't stripped enough of it through the guides and had been trying to cast the weightless leader—a mistake an absolute novice would make.

I stopped a moment, thinking of how long it had been since I really fished, with all my concentration, with all my soul, with the rod and line as the divining stick of my passion about rivers and trout.

Years.

So many other passions had intruded and taken over: climbing, photography, hunting, horses. And then there was the business of the fish themselves. It is hard not to notice, at some point, that fish don't like being taken out of the water, that they do their best not to be winched toward land, which indeed is why we like to catch them. They fight.

Some of us notice this with the first few fish that we catch and give up fishing entirely. Others of us, who are so enthralled by fish as the symbols of the natural world from which we have parted, symbols that we can touch and let go and touch again, never realize or manage to forget that fish have no similar feelings. I had been in this latter group of anglers for a long time—

since I was a boy. But the more fish I caught and let go (and we're talking thousands of fish, all over the world, and over decades of my life), the less satisfying the activity became. Not that I had ever addressed the question of why fishing had become less satisfying. It just had become less compelling, and I left it at that. Other activities replaced angling in importance, it's true, but the real reason was that I became increasingly uncomfortable with the knowledge that addressing the question of whether fish feel pain, addressing it in a rigorous way, would lead me into country that I didn't want to know.

During the last few years, when I did occasionally still fish and actually caught something, I bopped the trout over the head and had a meal, which continued to seem forthright and somehow equal: You, trout, eat bugs and worms and other trout, and I, human, eat you. Since the trout did not rise to its prey and spit it out and catch it again and again, which is what catch-and-release sportfishing is all about, I reasoned that neither should I. At the heart of the matter this was why, in the last decade, I had fished less and hunted more. The hunting, which had to do with food gathering and not sport, sat easier in my soul.

Getting the line stripped through the guides, I tried another cast, the rod moving through the air, the line loading and un-loading it, and hissing neatly. Like riding a bike, the motion came back quickly. I tapped the rod above the spot that I wanted the fly to hit, a green delta of water below a small cascade of foam, and it landed almost there. In small bites, I stripped in line and cast again.

The line landed, floated, and darted. Before I could respond to the strike, the trout flashed through the pool, bowing the rod. Bringing the small fish in easily, I slipped my hand under it. It jumped and the barbless hook flew into the air.

Perfect, I thought, looking into the pool where the brown trout had disappeared, and then at the tiny nymph hanging on the end of my leader, amazed that it had all happened again: my knowing that the fish was just behind the spume-charged water, then dropping this little bit of hair above the spot, and predicting, almost to the millisecond, when the hit would come.

I felt a calmness settle through me, which is not only the calmness of a job well done but also the calmness that comes from being able to predict and control events. I walked upriver, taking a fish from every flume and also casting to the wide and shallow places, even though I knew that there were no fish there. It was just so lovely to watch the line unwind and alight and float upon the placid water, as if the line were the graph of my soul, gone even and smooth after the disconcerting tour of the mine site.

And I began to remember the sounds as well as the biomechanical pleasures of fly-fishing: the crisp snap of line against the spool when I had stripped just enough coils for the cast; how by throwing a rollcast upstream I could unhook the nymph snagged on rocks; how, sidearm, I could throw a cast beneath a downstream gust of wind; or how, by moving the rod over my head, I could change directions in mid-cast. And nothing went awry because I kept the line short, doing just what I could handle and walking up to the pools instead of throwing at them from afar. It was all so lovely, there in the light of September, the aspens blowing and whispering, the water tugging at my legs and spraying my arms, that I felt my chest swell and break apart, like clouds before the sun.

An ouzel jumped from boulder to boulder; a kingfisher swept across the river; far upstream, a cow elk came down to the water's edge and drank. Merle, who had been standing patiently in the water, and who likes to hunt more than fish, looked at her and looked at me and seemed to say, "Why are you wasting your time standing in this river?"

Climbing up the small, ankle-deep falls, wading slowly across the shallow pools, and casting to the narrow channels, I caught a dozen fish, some of them LDRs—long-distance releases, a phenomenon in which the fish, leaping at the end of thirty feet of line, throws the nymph back at the angler, bypassing the task of actual releasing. Other trout I brought to hand, held a moment, and slipped back into the current.

There was one more pool, then the river flattened into the upper meadows. I cast several times into the pool, which lay half in shadow, half in fractured, glittering light, letting the nymph circulate into all the deep crannies. The line dove. When I raised the rod, the fish was solid, as if I had hooked a rock. Then it flashed out of the pool and I followed it downstream, guiding it through a narrow channel before bringing it in. It made two more runs before I could grab it.

It was one of those perfectly symmetrical trout: husky, full of strength and color, and long as my forearm. And I could have killed it, because in this stretch of the Lewis you can kill fish. And I thought about it, thought about declaring that I had really been hunting for a meal today and that this trout would be a fine meal. But I hadn't been hunting at all and hadn't really fished that way for years, if I had ever done so at all. I had fished as recreation, as competition with my cousin, and as an excuse to visit wild places because I didn't know that I could go someplace and just look at wildlife or climb over mountains and still come home happy without having to reach a high lake containing fish. When I did realize that I didn't have to fish to enjoy a place, I still continued to do it out of inertia and because people were willing to pay me to fish, to write about it, and to photograph it. It is diffi-

cult, until you harden your principles, to turn down trips to remote and singularly beautiful places that you'll never get to any
other way.

I had also used fishing as the social oil between friends and,
throughout the years, as a way to stroke my ego, looking for, finding, and landing ever bigger fish on ever lighter tackle. Today, I
had used fishing as a way to mollify my depression concerning
the mine—to find some peace in a beautiful place by skillfully
casting line and seeing lovely fish come up through the lens of
the river and into my sun-dappled world. Which, OK, is better
than taking Prozac for getting over the blues but shouldn't be
confused with what a trout does when it rises to a mayfly.

That moment of predation—kill to eat to be alive (not psy-
chically or spiritually alive, but biologically alive, the kind of
alive that calories sustain)—is how I liked to think that I hunted
when I hunted for elk or grouse. I enjoyed the pursuit, the physical demands, and the mental discipline, solving problems of
time and distance and cutoff angles, of being silent for hours—
the way I have seen wolves enjoy stalking and chasing elk or
caribou—but I don't believe that I've used a grouse's pain or an
elk's pain to fill something else beside my stomach and my sense
of doing a hard job well. In my life hunting, I hadn't tried to kill
animals with larger and larger antlers as, in my life fishing, I had
tried to land ever larger fish; nor had I adopted the challenges of
handicapping equipment—using, say, muzzleloaders or archery
to introduce a new frisson into what had become a well-worn
activity—in the way I had been willing to constantly recalibrate
the thrills of angling by using ever-lighter tackle, so that a two-
pound trout on a one-weight rod became the sensory equivalent
of a six-pound trout on a five-weight rod. In the process of becoming more technically proficient in angling, I had permitted

myself to forget that on the end of my line was a creature who was fighting for its life. Never had I forgotten that about birds and mammals—one doesn't "play" them as one does fish, and their pain is too apparent to discount. Certainly, I had never tried shooting them as an analgesic for the environmental equivalent of a bad-hair day.

There has always come a moment when, hiding, I can no longer hide, when my throat and chest constrict with the knowledge that I've been avoiding a hard-to-face truth. It has been this way since I was a boy.

I let the trout go, let this lovely Lewis River trout go with a sense of letting go a life—mine as well as his. I walked up the bank and sat in the grass. Looking down the river, I wished that I was still a boy, that I could still happily catch and release fish and that it would always be the beginning of September, with the mountains, my once-private mountains, still quiet and empty.

CATCH and DENY

Jack Turner, who looks like a cross between a jolly medieval monk and the Buddha, gave up trout fishing because of birds.

"It was in Berkeley," he says, "maybe '88 or '89. I heard this recording done by the Royal Academy or someone like that. It was of fish being caught and trying to escape. You didn't have to be an expert to know that these were creatures in distress. The only thing I could think of was birds."

It's after dinner, and we're standing on the town square of Jackson, Wyoming, which is virtually empty because it's April and off-season. Turner, one of the principal guides at the Exum School of Mountaineering, based just north of town in Grand Teton National Park, wears his usual tweedy coat, T-shirt, and shortly trimmed white beard, making him look both weathered and wise. Besides having led hundreds of climbers up the Grand Teton, Turner is also known for his mountain explorations (he was the first American to reach the north side of K2), his retrospects of the early days of Yosemite climbing, and lately his lyric writings on everything from Buddhism to the lives of white pelicans. He has also been a fishing junkie since the age of four.

"Trout, eels, everything," he says. His grandfather was half-owner of a Pennsylvania fishing and hunting lodge, and Turner grew up with a rod in his hand before turning to the mountains and teaching philosophy. It was his bent for philosophy, for making unusual connections and disquieting comparisons, that finally caught up to him.

"When I first read defenses of catch-and-release fishing," he explains, "when it became really popular maybe fifteen years ago, I had my first inkling that I didn't want to do it. It seemed like a continuation of a utilitarian philosophy that maximizes value for the group and ignores the individual. It's the perennial scientific attitude as well. Biologists don't worry about individuals. They worry about species, ecosystems.

"Then I heard that recording and it made me imagine using worms and flies to catch mountain bluebirds or pine grosbeaks, or maybe eagles and ospreys, and hauling them around on fifty feet of line while they tried to get away. Then when you landed them, you'd release them. No one would tolerate that sort of thing with birds. But we will for fish because they're underwater, out of sight."

Sometime after listening to the recording, Turner sold his fishing gear—Winston rods mounted with Hardy reels, the best of fine trout tackle. "It breaks my heart to talk about it," he says flatly.

The renunciation was too much too soon. He bought back his rods, used them for two more seasons, and couldn't stand how he felt about what he was doing to fish. He sold everything again. Even so, he's not sure the sale is final.

"I may buy back my nine-foot-six Winston and go out for a trout dinner, or catch whitefish for a stew, going out with the idea specifically to hunt a fish to eat it. I'm not opposed to hunting—

killing fish for food. In fact, I don't think hunting to eat is immoral—to go out, for instance, with a shotgun to kill a dove and eat it—because all life survives by killing and consuming other life. But this idea of playing with things for our own enjoyment while they go through great anguish and suffering strikes me as wrong."

Turner is a member of a Zen Buddhist school that doesn't value life-forms by their sentience. Insects, shrimp, cows, people, trees, rocks, and mountains "all deserve our care and attention." He does, however, distinguish between instrumental and gratuitous pain—killing a fish to feed your gut and playing with a fish to feed your ego.

He now throws open his hands, taking in the town square, the valley, and places beyond. "As a culture we're addicted to fun," he says, "and have a hard time placing amusement in a secondary place to other values, the good of the environment for instance, or the suffering of other beings, even when we recognize those values as important."

Turner isn't alone in feeling uncomfortable about catch-and-release fishing. A few days later, I'm in Montana, talking with David Quammen, whose quirky and poetic essays on nature have appeared in *Outside* for years. Like someone going through a divorce or a serious illness, I'm looking for a support group, people who have lived and lusted for fishing and are now going through the same sort of withdrawal that I've been experiencing.

Quammen and I sit in the old Chico Hot Springs Lodge, commanding a bench above the Yellowstone River where it meanders through Paradise Valley. It's one of those April evenings when the last bit of warm sun makes you believe that winter is really coming to a close. As with Turner, I ask Quammen the question that no one in the fishing world really likes addressing because of the Pandora's box it opens: If fish do feel pain, as some evidence has begun to suggest, what does the catch-and-release angler do with that knowledge?

Quammen, whose writings explore the givens of nature and the ambiguities of the human soul, answers slowly, almost tortuously, as if mirroring the hard journey he's traveled while thinking about this subject. "I've had more and more trouble with catch-and-release fishing as time goes on. I haven't stopped completely . . . and I haven't decided that one shouldn't fish," he adds quickly, making sure I understand that he's not about to offer any moral prescriptions. "But I've concluded that it's speciesist to tell ourselves that it's a game to the fish. It's deadly mortal serious to them. These animals were hysterically fighting for survival, and it didn't matter whether you had your barbs bent down."

He pauses. His black shirt, flowered tie, and long hair pulled back in a ponytail make him look like a rock musician or an eccentric physicist. This is a man who once criticized cougar hunting in print, then, several years later, at the invitation of a cougar hunter who wrote him about the flaws in his argument, accompanied the man and his dog through Montana's mountains. Eventually, Quammen ate a dinner of lion meat and wrote in another column, "Whatever arguments might be made against the hunting of mountain lions, inedibility isn't one of them." He also wrote, "Nor would I argue for any absolute ethical distinction between the killing of a mountain lion and the killing of a trout."

As a slogan, "catch and release" was first used in the early 1960s by Richard Stroud, the head of the Sport Fishing Institute, an organization funded by fishing-tackle manufacturers. It almost immediately replaced what fish and game departments had been calling "fishing for fun," a phrase coined in the late 1950s by Albert Hazzard, the assistant executive director of the Pennsylvania Fish Commission, for a program of catching trout and putting them back in Clinton County's Old Woman's Creek. As Stroud recalls, "I gave a speech in which I said, 'I don't like the term "fish for fun." All fishing is fun. So I'll use the term "catch and release." ' "

If inventing a byword insures immortality, Stroud's future is secure. In terms of societal recognition, "catch and release" is right up there with "thermos" and "Scotch tape." What "catch and release" doesn't address, of course, is "incidental kill"—the 5 to 10 percent of the trout that die from stress no matter how carefully they're handled. Warm-water fish, such as bass, suffer ever-higher rates of incidental kill. Least addressed in both the popular and professional literature is whether fish—caught and killed fish or caught and released fish—feel pain during the process. Which is Michael K. Stoskopf's whole point.

Stoskopf's easiness belies the enormity of his message. He is a department head at the College of Veterinary Medicine at North Carolina State University in Raleigh. Today, he has flown across the country to speak at the annual meeting of the Colorado Wildlife Society in Fort Collins. Stoskopf's late-in-the-day presentation is a summary of a paper he authored called "Pain and Analgesia in Birds, Reptiles, Amphibians, and Fish." Of the 14,406 references to fish that he surveyed in the literature, only twenty-four matched fish and pain; of those, nineteen were about pain in humans caused by diseases contracted from fish. Of the remaining five references, none discussed the fact that fish might actually feel pain. Stoskopf concluded that the scientific community, like the public, has a serious misconception.

"Pain and pain perception in nonmammalian species must be unimportant," he says, "or at least so intrinsically different from the process in mammals that we need not apply our basic knowledge of mammalian nociception to birds, reptiles, amphibians, or fishes." But when Stoskopf applied basic knowledge of mammalian nociception—the ability to react to painful or injurious stimuli—to nonmammals, he found that they exhibited the four basic responses that mammals do: rapid startle reactions; simple nonspecific flight; vocalization; and "coordinated reaction," a bit of jargon meaning that the test individual bites the source of pain.

As for fish, they not only exhibited "pronounced reactions to contact with irritants or acute stimuli, including strong muscular and behavioral avoidance" (what makes our fishing reels sing their arias when we haul a fish toward shore), but they also showed unfamiliar responses such as color changes and subtle alterations in posture and in the habitats that they chose. The biochemical evidence for pain perception in fishes was also hard to discount: The nervous systems of teleosts (bony fishes that include trout and salmon) produced compounds related to those that mammals produce when subjected to pain.

Turning off his slide projector, Stoskopf smiles at the glum audience. "As you might suspect," he says, "these findings have profound implications for the fishing community, especially the catch-and-release segment of that community, which bills its sport as qualitatively different and somehow less injurious than hunting." Though his words make him seem antifishing, he isn't. "The danger," he explains, "is being in denial about what you're doing and then finding yourself in an indefensible position.

"It's also not bad to have fun," he adds with a grin, "because a lot of the economy's power to implement important habitat benefits comes from people enjoying themselves. That may mean inflicting pain in a variety of ways to individuals. It benefits the species, and it's certainly different from being cruel."

When told of Stoskopf's data, people like Ted Williams go ballistic. "I don't believe it," he says, voice rising. The conservation editor for *Fly Rod and Reel* and a take-on-anyone columnist for *Audubon,* Williams regularly infuriates both the left and the right. Trying to keep his tone level, he says, "I've caught bluegills off their nests four and five times within an hour. If it hurt them that bad they wouldn't be behaving this way." Williams is tired and disgusted with this entire discussion. "Needless guilt and contemplating our navels," he calls it. Then he says, "It's as simple as this. I'm a person, it's a fish. A friend likened catch-and-release fishing to lassoing a white-tailed deer and hauling it in until it's exhausted. But it's not analogous. If we're going to believe that, we should apply it further. We shouldn't be putting DEET on our skin because it disrupts the feeding activity of mosquitoes."

"But the deer analogy is about deriving pleasure from another's pain, while putting DEET on is to stop someone from hurting us," I reply. Long pause. "I guess so," he says, searching for another comparison. "It's like the Puritan sex ethic. Sex is only good if you don't enjoy it."

Before I mention that enjoyable sex is usually between consenting partners, Williams lets fly with catch and release's broadside. Citing the story of the threatened greenback cutthroat trout living in Rocky Mountain National Park, he turns our discussion to the issue of species and habitat preservation. The greenback cutthroat trout was originally listed as "endangered," but its recovery program "went nowhere," he says, "because no one could fish for it." Downlisting the trout to "threatened" and allowing catch-and-release fishing for it created a constituency. Money poured in and greenbacks increased.

This story has now become a classic and powerful ecological justification for catch-and-release fishing. It also doesn't stand by itself. After catch-and-release regulations were instituted on Yellowstone Lake and its feeder streams in 1973, cutthroat trout numbers increased as much as fourteen times in some of the creeks, creating profound ripple effects. In 1975, grizzly bears fished for cutthroats in 19 percent of the lake's feeder streams; by 1980, the bears were using 61 percent of the streams, an increase that John Varley, director of the Yellowstone Center for Resources and a man whom Williams likes to quote, attributes directly to catch-and-release regulations. Later, when I talked with Varley at park headquarters in Mammoth Hot Springs, he said, "If eagles and ospreys and grizzly bears and otters were going to vote on catch and release as opposed to catch and kill, we would get unanimous support for the former."

"We need to be saving habitat," Williams repeats, echoing Varley, "not worrying whether the cutthroat likes being pulled in and released." Having fired his big guns on the habitat issue, Williams now makes a conciliatory gesture. "The people who say we need to kill fish and eat them, they are absolutely right, absolutely. When I was on the Thorne River, one of America's ten most endangered, by the way, because of logging, I was walking along the stream bank one morning. I heard what I thought was a rattlesnake. It was a coastal cutthroat jumping in the air and shaking its fins. Feeding on pink salmon fry. Hot fish right out of the cold Pacific. The first one I caught jumped five times and broke me off. And all we had brought for breakfast were sticky buns, and by God it was pretty nice to kill a couple of those cutthroats and fry them in butter and eat them. If we hadn't done that, that fishing experience wouldn't have been as powerful for us. And we released about fifteen that we didn't kill."

His voice becomes reflective. He's getting to the denouement, what really counts for him. "The reason I've stayed with catch and release is—it's not the fight. It's seeing the fish come up, sip the fly. Just to see that. It's pretty neat. Being in Yellowstone is being part of the ecosystem, watching the flies dimple the water, looking at the sky. I don't go to fight them. I go to join them."

If that's it—just wanting to be part of things as Williams and the rest of us have claimed—why not clip off the bend of the hook and simply cast the harmless fly?

John Betts, the renowned flytier and angling scholar, not only thought of the question before I did, he thought of the answer. Disturbed by the small but inevitable percentage of trout injured while being released, Betts began to fish with flies from which the hook bends had been cut. Trout would rise to these hookless flies three, four, even half a dozen times. Damage to the fish was zero, but Betts was disappointed. "Missing was the adrenaline surge that came from the anticipation, take, and initial runs and jumps," he wrote in *American Angler*, a journal devoted to fly-fishing and fly-tying.

Still needing some connection with the fish, albeit brief, Betts started to tie "tag" hooks, standing for "touch and go." They have a ringed eye at both ends. The business end can't penetrate the fish's mouth but will hold the fish long enough for the angler to feel it on the end of his or her line, see it jump, maybe even get a run or two out of it. "My need to touch whatever I've caught," Betts reflected, "originated in lessons learned millions of years ago for reasons other than sport. Touching is one of the last vestiges of our past and may now seem our only way to keep in contact with it. It also provides a sense of validity for ourselves at the moment and later, when we tell others about what we've done. My need to touch is now tempered by the realization that resources are limited and that what I touch is becomingly increasingly scarce."

Betts's little essay generated a loud response. Half of the letters to the editor offered a variation on "Kudos for this courageous article." Half said, "Let me puke." Most people entirely missed Betts's point about how catch-and-release fishing is being used to provide angling in a time when most places have quite literally run out of fish.

Not far from where Betts fishes on Colorado's South Platte River, another angler, Bob Behnke, professor of fishery biology at Colorado State University, ponders many of the same questions, particularly the biblical one of transforming few fish into many to feed the hungry masses. His work and his popularization of others' research has undermined two popular angling myths—namely, that barbless hooks are necessary for successful catch-and-release fishing and that the single hook is less injurious than the treble hooks used on spinning lures. Behnke cites controlled studies in which mortality did not increase with barbed hooks or with treble ones. Such evidence infuriates the purists with their hat brims studded with expensive flies, their barbs bent down.

People in the animal-rights movement are also angry at Behnke, for he maintains that fish don't experience the sort of pain that a human might experience with a hook in its mouth. "If it *was* an experience of extreme trauma, comparable to a human's being taken to a hospital after a severe injury," he says, "you would not likely do it again within a day. Yet you can catch the same fish every day by dangling a lure in front of it. Cutthroats are caught and released about ten times each season in the Yellowstone River within the park. They would learn not to be caught again if they were experiencing extreme pain."

He does note that cutthroats are notoriously easy to catch as compared to brown trout, with rainbows ranked someplace between the two species. Do brown trout thus feel more pain than cutthroats do? Or are they just smarter?

Since fish can't tell us about what they're feeling, Behnke suggests that we have to make inferences about their pain thresholds from circumstantial evidence. Citing electroshock sampling methods, used across the nation by fishery biologists to gather information about trout populations, he says, "Those fish are hit again and again, several times in one year, with electric shock that makes them stiff as a board. We know that the shock causes hemorrhaging and fracturing of the vertebrate column. But as far as the trout's continued survival and growth, there's no indication that the shocking is damaging them. Some of our most famous trout waters would never support the numbers of trout they do if electroshocking were really harming the fish.

"Or take tagging," he goes on, "where numbered tags are inserted with wires right through the fish's body with no evidence that it's harming their survival, growth, or well-being. In fact, they carry these tags for years. Or here's another example of the difference between fish and humans: In coastal waters, salmon are routinely attacked by sea lions; you see the fish swimming upstream with wounds that would be lethal to a person."

But what about Stoskopf's contention that fish feel pain because their physiological reactions to stress are similar to those of mammals? "Similarities don't mean that they're feeling the same kind of pain," Behnke counters. Then, like Williams, he points out that whether individual fish actually feel what we know as pain is really not the issue we should be discussing. "Catch and release is a management tool. Without catch and release you wouldn't be able to maintain quality fishing."

Lee Wulff, indisputably one of the greatest fly anglers of this century, said the same thing more simply in 1939: "Game fish are too valuable to be caught only once." From a biological, political, and economic standpoint such reasoning can't be faulted. Catch and release maintains fish populations and pleases anglers. Anglers vote and they buy fishing licenses, helping to keep fish and game departments in business. They also buy tackle and clothing, stay in motels, eat in restaurants. There isn't a chamber of commerce in the land that weighs a fish's pain against its community's annual revenues.

You have to seek out someone like Jack Turner to see the crack in this utilitarian armor. "We're dealing with a group of people," he says, "fishermen, climbers, boaters, for whom fun and sport are more important than virtually anything else and who lack restraint. We could further limit access to the resource. Maybe have a lottery like in the Grand Canyon. Raise the cost of licenses. We don't have to give everyone unlimited fishing opportunities. Maybe this is something that can't be done everyplace. But it could be done in Yellowstone and Grand Teton parks, which already prohibit river running. Ultimately, people will have to restrict their use of nature."

When I point out to Turner that this would turn America into Europe, where only the wealthy get to fish for trout (and where trout are killed and eaten), he sighs. His calling is principles, not politics.

The rivers clear, the summer warms and turns to fall. I digest—not trout but ideas about trout. Like everything else in nature, these beautiful fish, their backs like fields of wildflowers, stand not for themselves but as an interface between humans and the primal world.

Not a single one of us has to catch a trout to eat. Nor, for that matter, do those of us who hunt big animals like moose or elk and feed our families for a year have to kill them to survive. We're making choices—more spiritual than economic—about grounding our souls in landscape through participation, about becoming participatory citizens of a home place through the eating of what that landscape produces. The wading, the casting, the stalking, the picking, the plowing, are the ceremonial means to procure nature's Eucharist.

I wade up the Gros Ventre River, my home river, as it flows out of its canyon and debouches before the Tetons. Year after year, it continues to produce as many whitefish as cutthroats, but this evening, the sun slanting onto the canyon walls, the water a deep malachite green, I hook neither. Still, I'm out again, trying to resolve my feelings about angling.

I wade upstream, between the silver flumes, hearing the rush of the water and immersed in spray, and loving the feel of the line—its tumescent load and spring, load and spring—as I cast. Everyone who talks about the catching of fish being secondary is right: simply being in the river is sensuous enough.

Almost enough.

If it were just the casting, the noise of the falling water, and the slanted evening light, there would be no reason to put a fly on the end of the line. We could just wade and cast. Few do. Most of us want a connection to the wild heart of the river, even if it is no more tenuous than seeing the fish come up to a hook-less fly—the heart of the heart of the river made manifest in its most essential gesture: stalking and eating prey. After all, trout are essential in the way we cannot be. They live seamlessly within their homes, within their actions, and within their brains. They are not removed. Maybe catching them, even only hooking them, allows the angler to enter their pure state of being for a moment, the nonreflective alpha and omega of existence. It is what well-practiced hunting and fishing are all about—focusing one's attention until the awareness of attention disappears.

The beauty of catch-and-release fishing, in an age that has grown dubious about causing harm to other life-forms, is that it focuses that attention without dire consequences to the creatures toward whom that attention is directed (at least 90 percent of the time, when the species is a cold-water one like trout and the fish is released quickly, in the water).

When we consider that we're products of a century that has spawned many legal manifestations of justice to the unempowered—woman's suffrage, citizenship for Indians, civil rights legislation, the Endangered Species Act, and global human rights—the action of releasing subdued fish resonates deeply in our psyches. Releasing what we have caught, we can then indulge ourselves in all the uplifting emotions of the kind steward's noblesse oblige—the shackled is set free and, in freedom, gives life to other residents of the ecosystem; grizzly bears and eagles. In economic terms, this is a "trickle up" effect. What is good for the trout is also good for the environment, and, no small benefit, good for the angler's soul since the actual death of the fish is perpetrated by another creature.

The tip of my line darts. I lift the rod in a gesture now practiced since I was a boy, and the weight of the fish is sudden, absolute, and amazingly sweet. The cutthroat splashes across the pool and rolls on the surface, the little reel singing like a diva. For half a minute, I just hold the trout because I'm using a two-pound-test tippet and the fish is nearly that big.

Finally, the fish tires and I pump it closer, letting the rod and the current do the work. After one more short run, I coax the fish close and bring my hand under its belly. Tucking the rod under my arm, I slide my hand down the leader and pause. After a whole year of thinking about these fish and talking to people who think about these fish (who actually think about these fish more than they do about a massacre in Rwanda or Bosnia), I should bop it on the head and take it home to eat. I should because I believe to the bottom of my soul that taking responsibility for some of the deaths we cause by our eating is one of the key elements of right living.

But I flick the hook out of the corner of its mouth (despite Behnke's evidence, I bent down the barb) and let it swim away. I don't want to keep it. Nor am I comfortable with letting it go. I head toward the shore, thinking, admitting that, in the end, we angle because we like the fight—otherwise all of us would be using hookless hooks. Not one angler in ten thousand does. The hook allows us to control and exert power over fish, over one of the most beautiful and seductive forms of nature, and then, because we're nice to the fish, releasing them "unharmed," we can receive both psychic dispensation and blessing. Needless to say, if you think about this relationship carefully, it's not a comforting one, for it is a game of dominance followed by cathartic pardons, which, as a nonfishing friend remarked, "is one of the hallmarks of an abusive relationship."

Hooking the fly into the line keep, I step onto the rocky bank. No one likes to hear his friends make those allusions about his fishing, especially when they have the slight ring of truth and especially after one has spent most of his life catch-and-release fishing. Hiking up the bank, my old waders leaking water, I wish I could lay it all to rest as easily as one of my neighbors, Yvon Chouinard, does. "You know fish feel some pain," said the old mountaineer turned master angler when I raised the issue with him, "because when you set the hook they explode. But they keep on striking," he explained, "so I think it's no big deal."

His voice gaining the slightest edge of discomfort, he added, "Shit . . . causing pain. If you want to know about pain, go run a marathon. Not all pain is negative. Not that these fish seek out pain, but it's not bugging them."

It's as good an answer as any, if you can really believe it.

PRIVATE MOUNTAINS

Above the cabin, the three rivers head. I stood there once, at Union Pass, palms open to a thunderstorm, my fingers flicking rain to the country. Ever since then, I've thought of the Colorado, the Missouri, and the Columbia as carrying my sweat.

The pass is a day's ride from the cabin, through the mountains that the French trappers called the Gros Ventre. Even so, it seems no more than "just above where I live," and all the collective wilderness surrounding it "my backyard." Maybe that's what being home is all about.

I ate rice and beans in the yellow lamplight of the kitchen while the September evening went mauve above the still-leafed cottonwoods. Then I cleared the table and laid out the reloading tools, the bullets like lined-up ingots, the powder like grain, swooshing through a funnel. When the twenty cartridges were done, I boxed them, stored the dies and hammer, and stepped into the living room with the rifle.

Above the stove is a knot, and I threw the gun and scope up to this makeshift bull's-eye and called five shots, the bolt making its slick fast slither between each tiny "click." Another, smaller knot took five more shots from the sitting position, and then the rifle went into its scabbard by the door, under the pile jacket, under the felt hat, above the waiting Sorels, covered with mud.

When I stepped outside, the crescent moon sat atop the Tetons. Faintly, a hush almost too soft to notice, the river coursed several fields away from the porch. Coyote yips jiggled along the far bank, and I looked up to Jupiter, thinking of how it is said that all our music originated as a form of deception used in hunting, that the Mbuti Pygmies and the Bushmen can, by singing, call birds and beasts within range of their arrows. Listening to the mountains, I could hear their hum, which made me feel as called, as lured within their range, as any eland or elk.

The next day, I ran up the hogbacks on the eastern side of the valley, liking the emptiness in my gut and how the parsnip and sedge brushed my legs. I imagined that this was what the elk must feel when they, too, strong and made lively by the cold, canter toward the sky.

In the afternoon, I put up targets on a hillside, shooting and tinkering with the scope until, at one hundred yards, I could cover my three bullet holes with a quarter. Back at home, I laid out the maps, five across and five deep on the living-room floor, and traced my fingers up the valleys and across the ridges, resting them at the hard-to-reach crests where remote streams headed and noting what economical routes connected these nodal points.

It grew late. I put the maps away, waterproofed my boots, installed a new pump in the stove, cleaned the binoculars, sharpened the skinning knife, packed two weeks of dry food for myself and oats for the horses, restocked their vet kit, and left a note on the kitchen table, to the friend who was to feed the cat, about where I intended to be and when I would be back. Then, with a smile, I thought that no one would ever know exactly where I'd be traveling for two weeks.

I damped down the fire and turned in, sleeping on the floor by my gear rather than in the bed upstairs. As my next-to-last thought I replayed the debate of this fall: whether I would take an animal just for the freezer or also try for what I had always considered a desire too filled with ego—a set of large and beautiful antlers. My last thought was that I also wanted the antlers—at least once and as a totem for this house, a reminder of all the elk who have built me, not only as food but as spirit, icons of home to be thanked and worshiped.

"Fishgait" was what I called his walk. Black as the four-thirty morning through which we climbed, Fish put his hooves down like a trout slipping through a flume—delicately. The frozen willows brushed his shoulders and moonlight shone on the orb of his left eye. Orion floated over the ridge above our camp. Looking at him, I wondered how, out of this improbable pattern of stars, the ancients had invented a celestial hunter. Perhaps they knew as cultures what we sense only as scattered individuals: that one always hunts beneath other eyes.

Fish and I continued up the unnamed mountain and glassed the parks where Grizzly, Bull, and Split Rock creeks meet. Color seeped into the gray meadows, and the shadows at the edge of tree line became nothing more than stumps. At sunrise we rode to a col that overlooks the valley of the Snake River. Sitting in the saddle, I watched the clear sunlight come across the continent and hit the Tetons, which I've known for sixteen actual years but which seem to own me from another lifetime.

They rise close to seven thousand feet from the valley floor, holding snowfields between their jagged spires and, lower down, gorges where no one has settled. Maybe I love them because they make the weather, turning the sky into moving spirit, the horizon into booming song.

We weren't alone. Beneath Fish's hooves lay the hoofprints of elk. They, too, had stood here gazing, perhaps as pleased, awed, and at last more concerned about other matters as I.

I dismounted, tied Fish to a tree, and still-hunted down through the timber—which means not to be still but to move so slowly and carefully that it appears that you're not moving at all. A steep but pleasant ridge, deep in needles, led my feet through the spruce. Elk trails meandered from its summit to the valley floor and eventually took me to a knoll covered with dry elk pellets. I bugled for several minutes, and the silence that the woods returned, along with the old sign, signaled that the herds had left.

I crossed several ridges, following a compass bearing through the dark forest, and dropped into Grizzly Creek. In a patch of snow, I actually did find a bear print, its plantigrade outline, walking from heel to toe, so much like my own. Ursus was out here hunting, too.

In a broad meadow below the snow, I took a mid-morning siesta, feeling the contentment that comes from being alone in the wild. With an easy mind, I lay down on the grass, cradled my head on my jacket, and went to sleep.

Twenty minutes of snoozing was enough to dispel the drowsiness left over from the 3:30 A.M. rising; then I worked up the north slopes of the creek, heading toward the ridge where I had left Fish. At one point, slipping easy-footed through the deadfall, on a slope that must have been inclined at forty degrees, I wondered if anyone else had stepped this way. After all, only another hunter would have had cause to traverse this forest, which lay on a route between nothing and nowhere. Indeed, from my vantage point, I had no vantage and hardly any footing. Perhaps, I thought, feeling a little charge of pleasure, I was the very first to walk here. Then I realized that, more important than being first, was the fact of being alone—that the world had been reduced to my solitary consciousness, and that in varying degrees, we all need this sort of space, this bubble of privacy around us. I thought of my bubble going twenty miles out to the Tetons and down into the Wind Rivers, and up into the Absarokas and felt happy that I had room to roam.

Within two weeks I wasn't happy. Though I had ridden and hiked from before dawn until after dark, I hadn't seen a single elk. Nor had I seen fresh sign. In fact, I had heard only two bugles. The first was that of a young spike, who whistled sharply at dusk but refused to answer my call. The second came as I returned to camp on another evening. My bugle was answered immediately and so loudly that I ran in a wide circle around my horse pasture, crawled to the blowdown behind my tent, raised my rifle, and peered over the top. Three men in orange—clutching rifles and grunt tubes—stared down the valley, toward where I had bugled. I was too embarrassed to do anything but slink away.

Then it snowed as if the country had decided to skip the foreplay of autumn and get down to the business of winter immediately. I moved camp close to the Continental Divide and tracked a bull through knee-deep snow for an entire morning before he walked across the north fork of Fish Creek and into an area whose season didn't open until October 1.

In the evenings, after feeding the horses and myself, and while lying in the stove-warmed tent, I would read *Bugle*, the quarterly journal of the Rocky Mountain Elk Foundation. One article told me that in 1985 only 16.88 percent of the elk hunters in

North America took home meat. Feeling as if I were being told to go home and take up bowling, I blew out the candle and slipped deeper into my sleeping bag. Then, as the wind blew snow against the door, my bouts of second-guessing continued: Why did you come out here alone? Why are you so damned concerned with challenge and doing everything yourself?

I had recently moved back to Wyoming from Colorado, after grad school, after much mountaineering and traveling and photographing in foreign places and after not hunting for several years and feeling out of practice. It would have been easy, I thought in one of those down-in-the-dump moods, to have hired an outfitter, someone who really knew the current movement of elk and could have put me on to some animals or, failing that, whom I could have blamed for my failure.

Yes, how much easier to answer the phone a month from now, hear a friend ask, "How did you do?" and say, "Why, I went out with Hearty Jim Bucko, the renowned Wyoming outfitter, and he said it was the worst elk season he's seen in all his born days." Instead, I would have to admit, "I didn't see a thing," and know my friends would be thinking that I must be getting old.

The next morning, when the country east of the divide opened to hunting, I rode into the broad basin of Papoose Creek and almost immediately found fresh tracks in the snow. Fish and I trailed them at a trot across several parks, and as they climbed toward Lava Mountain I spurred Fish on. Where the going became too steep for a horse, I left him and climbed quickly through the spruce, jumping over fallen logs, breathing hard at ten thousand feet, and feeling full of oxygen, coursing blood, and adrenalin. In a windblown meadow, the tracks became spare, but I found them again at the tree line. Kneeling, I touched some urine, which was still warm. I slowed to a crawl, smelling success just ahead and—suddenly—the reek of musk on a draft of air. Stealth became my name, a frame a second my pace, while my lungs ached with the effort of controlling my panting. I took a minute to step over a blowdown, hearing, as my boot came down, the compaction of the snow make the tiniest "phumpf." The forest exploded with breaking timber. Hoofbeats went down a gully, others circled me, and two cows stopped short and eyed me from thirty yards. Seeming to know they were safe—I had only a bull license—they took small steps and made a slow retreat.

Within twenty yards, I found the bull's tracks, which dove off a small, ideally situated knoll with a view in every direction. His downhill tracks never left a gallop, and though I followed him for hours, I knew I'd never catch up. Suddenly, I felt tired—too many 3 A.M. mornings. I also felt ill—perhaps it was depression. I rode Fish to camp, packed, and that afternoon left him and my packhorse, Verle, at the stable on Togwotee Pass. I slunk back home.

Hoping to find a bolstering word or maybe a check in the mail, I stopped in front of the post office and opened the door quietly. The hinge of my box made a squeak and Lee, the postman, looked up from his newspaper and peered out from the mail slot behind which he sits.

"Got a big one strapped to your car?"

"Nope."

"Too bad," he said, and added, "It's a bad season."

The wildlife officer in town agreed—"funny September"—as did the cashier in the grocery store, the teller in the bank, and a ranger in the park. I decided to take a vacation from elk. A couple friends from Lander and I drove to the eastern plains and consoled ourselves with filling our antelope tags. This put some meat in the freezer, and on my way back through Lander I also got in touch with some outfitter friends I knew, who said sure, we could go out during the last week of elk season. I told them I'd think about it. Their offer was extremely tempting, for when you come right down to it, the basic business of an elk hunt is to get an elk, and using the services of an outfitter seemed a fine way for an out-of-practice, down-in-the-dump hunter to ensure that.

I almost plugged myself into this equation, but something stopped me, and I guess that something was my underlying sentiment that hunting is a private passion. Certainly, you can argue that even when going with a guide, it's the hunter himself who presses the trigger. Yet the events leading to that moment—the camping, the walking, the wandering, and the doubts—are, by necessity, shared to varying degrees when two or more people hunt together. Sometimes this sharing creates a powerful union, occasionally even making strangers comrades. But at other times, the sharing of the burdens and the joys seems to detract from the private song that you're creating between yourself, the elk, and the mountains. And as for the outcome of this song—well, no one knows it until the very last day.

Having had to return the leased horses, I hunted from the cabin, driving out in the dark early mornings to hike the western slopes of the Gros Ventre and returning well after dark, usually covered to my knees in mud. By the end of October, I could no longer face the alarm. I woke when my body was ready, ate breakfast in the daylight, and wrote until afternoon. Toward three o'clock, I drove up Ditch Creek, parked the car at the road closure, and set off through the forest. Within fifteen minutes, I saw an ear flick, then the head of a cow moose. Not five minutes farther along, a doe and a buck bounded away. Near the ridge crest, I passed over some bear scat. Pleased with these signs of my neighbors, not far from the computer at which I wrote, I still-hunted along the edge of a long meadow and took a stand at its final crest, which overlooked the Tetons in one direction and rolling parks and forest in the other. The sun set, and I watched it for quite a while, finally remembering what had brought me here. I glanced back down the meadow, and there, as plain as anything could be, was a forkhorn elk.

The wind blew toward me; he quartered away, almost 450 yards away. At the distant tree line, he stopped and looked back, and I had a moment to put the crosshairs in the air over his spine. I couldn't sit down because of the tall grass, but, on paper, I had occasionally made such offhand shots. Studying his forked antlers one more time, and how far away he seemed, I pushed the safety forward, and I'm not sure that in the next instant I rationally examined the many strictures I had set for this elk hunt, or how far away I would actually shoot, or the ending to the story that I wanted to write, or, in more general terms, what might be called the "life myth" each of us creates for himself. In this myth, for this particular fall, the young elk walked into the forest, and I let him go. As I went down to the car, I wasn't unhappy.

On the evening before the last day of the season, it snowed. It snowed six inches on the valley floor, and because the snow would make for good tracking and because it was the last day, I rose at three-thirty and cooked some antelope sausage.

I took the Jeep because I reckoned the car would get stuck. Instead, the Jeep lost traction on the final curves and left me with an extra mile to walk up Ditch Creek. No tracks littered the meadow in which I had seen the forkhorn and so, as the sun rose, I walked on, continuing up to where the ridge fell away into the valley of the Gros Ventre. There, I sat on a rock and looked over the hills and dense morning clouds flowing like rivers down the valleys. Beyond the Gros Ventre, range after range of conifer forest stacked into the silver-and-yellow bands of sky in the east. I knew that I had hunted well, and I sensed that the land, in this moment of solicitude, agreed.

It's hard to disappoint that accord. Though I was tired, I continued on through the snow, traversing the headwaters of Tangled Creek. There, in a nasty, tree-choked gully, I picked up a couple of moose prints—cow and calf—and followed them only because they went in the general direction I was heading. By ten, I had crossed no other tracks. However, I had used up my morning's energy. In a park full of sunlight, I stopped for tea, nuts, and a nap.

After a half hour I woke, cleared the sleep from my eyes, and tried to decide where an elk would be on this last day of the season. Naturally, it was the question I had been asking myself for seven weeks. As ever, I answered it by surmising that an elk who didn't want to be seen was down in the timber. I dropped into the forest, going through small parks.

In the second meadow I crossed, I found five sets of tracks. They headed north, paralleling the Tetons standing sentinel to the west. I followed. Underfoot, the snow was soft; overhead, the sky was streaked with cirrus clouds, presaging more weather.

I tracked in and out of gullies for perhaps twenty minutes, then climbed a small ridge beyond which lay a steep park. The park was creased by a stream and held a copse of aspen. Some of the tracks led away from this meadow, and I turned and followed them for only fifty yards before noticing that they had reversed direction. Retracing my steps to the ridge and going one step farther over its crest than before, I spied four cow elk bedded in the aspen, about one hundred yards away.

Sinking into the snow next to the trunk of a spruce tree, I put my arm through the rifle's sling and waited. A minute went by.

Then the largest cow stood and, chewing methodically, stared at the tree under which I sat. In another minute all four cows stood and, following the matriarch's lead, began to walk slowly up the opposite hillside. There were conifers below the aspen grove, and out of this dark tangle came another cow, then a sixth, a seventh, and an eighth. I couldn't believe that there was no bull among so many cows. A ninth, tenth, and eleventh cow joined the line walking through my scope. The twelfth animal to emerge from the forest wore antlers, and the open slope must have worried him. Throwing back his head, he began to run, which set off the cows into a gallop.

I followed him through the veil of aspen, peeked over the scope and saw an opening. When he crossed it, I fired, and he lurched. He kept running, and I noticed the ejected shell fly out of the right corner of my vision, though I don't remember working the bolt. Then he was on the open hillside, and when the rifle came back hard, he went down, his legs kicking the snow.

I steadied the rifle butt on the ground, looked at the sky, and realized that it was all over. Then I noticed that my rifle barrel, gripped in my hand, was shaking. "Thank you," I said out loud, noticing that I had aimed my voice toward the horizon, where earth met sky, and in one of those sudden ahas I realized that over the years the direction of my prayers had come down a bit.

Slowly, not wanting the moment to end, I walked downhill to the beds of the elk and looked at the twelve kidney-shaped depressions in the snow, the air heavy with musk. Then I walked up the hillside, not seeing the bull for quite a while because he was just at the crest, and finally seeing his hind legs, which seemed too long to be real. I walked around him, realizing once again how large an elk is when you are next to him, and stood by his head before kneeling by his antlers, which had five points on each side. These I touched one by one, as well as his ears, and the thick hair on his forehead, and his still-wet and lovely nose.

I sat with him for a quite a while, wondering why he had chosen to follow his cows into the open rather than sneaking away through the timber, and knowing the answer. His park fell steeply into the valley, and I watched its descent—meadow and forest—until I thought I could remember it exactly, especially the Tetons, rising full of snow and silence as they have almost forever. He and I were part of that time and that song now.

I laid down his head. I took out my knife. It was long after dark before I reached the road.

LOGGING

In a valley of quiet, we empty the sky, felling trees with horses, among a circle of sweat and friends. Some would call this logging. I don't know what to call it: life? building a cabin? being a mindful citizen of my home? I search for a name, using my hands and teeth, my nose.

The tinkle of the bell mare drifts down the slope, the hand-turned winch clicks, the heady, musty smell of working horses mixes with the odors of spruce, sun-warmed resin, and huckleberries. Standing on the arch—the mobile winch that hoists one end of logs off the ground—Woody says "Back" to the two draft horses, their hooves the size of buckets. He wears a torn shirt and filthy jeans, gold-framed spectacles, and a hard hat shaped like the First World War helmets of American soldiers.

At his command, each horse takes a diminutive step backward, moving the arch into place. Woody wraps the horses' reins around a metal tender on the front of the arch, both of which he designed and welded, then jumps lightly from log to log like a marten, prying apart the trees with a pike and circling them with hook and chain. He moves with longtime practice and care.

Across the valley, the opposite hillsides rise to granite out-crops: meadow and aspen; meadow and conifers; meadow and sky, as empty and crystal blue as the sound of the bell. Here, on the north-facing side of Mosquito Creek, the fir and spruce rub branches, allowing only rough circles of light to pool on the for-est floor.

After helping Woody top off the load and watching him drop out of sight down the skid trail with the horses, I walk back among our cut, through an old stand of lodgepole pines whom we are about to fell. White of bark, straight, and tall, the trees have lost their green. However, unlike Yellowstone's lodgepole forest to the north, they've seen no fire. No life-giving holocaust has seared their trunks, providing a blaze to pop their dormant cones and start a new grove, the centuries-old story of this fire-dependent species. In the course of time, they've simply grown old, growing and growing until their trunks have fattened to six-teen, eighteen, twenty inches in diameter. Such trees are no more than sticks in the Pacific Northwest, but here, in the high moun-tains of Wyoming, they're not only good sized, but when it comes to lodgepoles, they're venerable. Woody has declared them the best house logs he's cut in the state.

Touching the trunk of the largest, I sight up to where its crown sways, slowly, gracefully, through the oh-so-blue sky. A slight breeze courses up there, eighty, a hundred feet off the ground. Down here, all is still. Once upon a time, the people who called this place home cut smaller lodgepoles into lengths of ten to twenty feet during the spring, peeled the bark, and set the poles aside. Come fall, the two-inch-thick trunks would have dried to a weight of only seven to ten pounds and would be stiff, strong, and virtually impossible to split. Lashed together and covered with buffalo hides, they formed the framework of a teepee, hence the name "lodgepole." The poles were also good for making a travois, which served as the means by which Plains Indians, journeying to the mountains for teepee fixings, dragged the bundled lodgepoles back to the prairies.

When the first settlers came to the Rockies, they used the lodgepole *(Pinus contorta)* for fencing corrals, and also for sheds, stables, and sometimes even for cabins, as I'm about to do. As the naturalist Donald Culross Peattie recounts in his great work, *A Natural History of Western Trees,* the species was also made into fruit boxes and telegraph and telephone poles. Bridge pilings, mine props, railroad ties . . . these, too, were once fashioned from this two-needled pine. In fact, across the next divide at Horse Creek, lumberjacks used to fell lodgepoles during the winter, saw them into six-foot lengths, trim them square with broadaxes, then stack them near the frozen streams. During the spring spate, these future railroad ties were floated to the Green River, boomed (held by cables stretched across the creek mouths), and floated south when the water reached its best height.

So today, up here in Mosquito Creek, we stand in a long line of loggers. I rub my palms against the tree, put my nose into its bark and inhale. Dry for years, it has lost its scent. Then I wrap my arms around its girth, measuring its bulk. Having counted the rings of trees already down, I know that this tree is a little over a hundred years old, which for the species is notable but not senescent. Four- to six-hundred-year-old individuals have been recorded. Still, compared to me this tree is an elder. It was a seedling before Wyoming became a state and before any white person homesteaded these valleys. It was already a little tree before my grandparents were born. It felt the ashes of the Mount Katmai and Mount Saint Helens eruptions fall on its needles and heard the silent mountains fill with the coming of trucks and atomic bombs and jets. It has witnessed the trapped-out beaver return and four generations of humans making deer and elk into meat. It has been present as these valleys were clear-cut and then reseeded, and now it is watching us take out the standing dead, of which it is one.

Even though our logging is selective and horse-drawn and completed in this circle of sweat and friendship, I'm not totally at ease with what we're doing, especially because the trees are old and ready to serve others besides me. Left alone, they might provide food and homes for sapsuckers, great horned owls, or a small bear. If I were a member of the family *Ursidae* instead of a human, such a fallen tree would be a delightful smorgasbord of ants and grubs and, excavated a little, also a snug winter den. Eventually, some of these trees would be split by lightning, others would be toppled by the wind; they would rot into soil.

I, however, am neither bird nor bear, and our species hasn't lived like these beings—seamlessly, totally within nature—for hundreds of thousands of years. Our logging will short-circuit this community's changing shape and going on as it has done for eons. This old tree will feel no rot, won't mingle its juices with the soil it has known. No sapsucker will tap on its trunk, no black bear fill its bole with soft hibernal breath. It will ride down the valley on Woody's flatbed truck and become the ridge log of my new house, hear the laughter of children, parents, and friends, listen to banjos and Beethoven, smell baking potatoes, Christmas pudding, and shampoo, watch moose and deer nose to its grovemates on the lower courses of the house, and feel ravens walk upon its back, as they once did here in Mosquito Creek. It will shelter my world—a sheltering that is, by my lights, as necessary as the sheltering of the bear. And I guess that the only way I can remain easy with its transformation from tree to human home is to be present as it happens, midwife as much as logger.

Above me, Tonio, Woody's helper this summer and also a naturalist from Costa Rica's Monteverde Cloud Forest, cajoles Milo, the huge chestnut gelding, backward toward a log. His voice, "Gee, haw, step," reminds me that I've been slacking off. Giving the tree a final pat, I begin to toss slash into piles, so that we'll have a clear trail to drag out the trees still to be cut. Four to six feet long, bristling with the jagged stumps of broken limbs, the slash needs both care and brute strength to move. I toss it downhill, wincing at what I'm crushing—willows, arnica, and beds of lush huckleberry—the bystanders and side-effect casualties of logging. But there is no clear spot of earth where the slash can be piled harmlessly. Vegetation covers the entire forest floor.

Those of us who divide the world into the sentient animal kingdom and the nonsentient plant kingdom might not give a second thought to crushing the undergrowth in this way as a by-product of logging—indeed, would never ascribe such anthropomorphic words as "seeing," "hearing," or "listening" to a lodgepole. By definition, the standing dead, as well as the live plants who inhabit our logging site and who are destroyed as we cut skid trails, can't have such faculties or feelings, since they are nonsentient, nonfeeling. Investing them with such capabilities, or even the sentience of the animal kingdom, is unscientific. If you are a writer and venture into this territory, you commit what the poet John Ruskin called "the pathetic fallacy."

This division, of course, is one way to understand the world. However, if you spend enough time outside, in landscapes that are quiet enough, you may begin to hear other voices. Listening to the pines respire, the aspen confabulate, and the cottonwoods complain, you begin to wonder if you are projecting your hopes and desires on the trees among which . . . (whom?) you walk. Are they mirroring your personality or do they have their own? If, too, the hillsides nod as you walk home after a day's work, saying, "Together we have passed and loved and created another day," if you hear the kindly whisper of grass and the hum of starlight as you fall asleep under the dark sky, if the world starts to speak—and by this I mean not actual words but body language, as dogs and cats and bears have body language that can be read—then it becomes more difficult to apply the term "non-sentient" to all those who are simply not ambulatory. When you let yourself touch the pain and sorrow of live animals and trees as they become food and wood for humans, participating in that great mystery of recombination in which life dies only to bring forth new life . . . when you put your hands up to the elbows into the womb of nature through fishing, farming, hunting, and logging and tenderly caress the place from where life springs, lamenting as well when it departs its current shape . . . then truly is it difficult to reduce the world neatly into the quick and the dead, the knowing and the unconscious.

Granted, I've never heard broccoli scream under my chef's knife, as one of my more sensitive vegetarian friends has, but it has been clear for a long, long time that not only do elk prefer to remain elk instead of becoming my flesh and blood, but so, too, would my potatoes prefer to remain in the ground than go into my microwave, and lodgepoles would prefer to continue thrusting their crowns to the sky instead of supporting my roof. This understory of vegetation, I'm certain, would choose, if it could, not to be converted prematurely into duff under a pile of slash.

For thousands upon thousands of years, other hunter-gatherers saw the plant and mineral kingdoms, not just the animal kingdom, as infused with spirit and consciousness. They asked the ash to allow itself to be made into a bow; they inquired of the mountain if it would allow them passage. The sky-centered religions of Judaism, Christianity, and Islam considered these people to be superstitious infidels and lost souls (although why talking to a mountain seems any more superstitious than talking to an invisible God in heaven has never made much sense to me). The Enlightenment, putting its faith in rational man, in progress and perfectibility, continued the disparagement of hunter-gatherers because such earth-centered people believed in processes that science could not verify with its instruments. We have continued that disparagement, doubting a Bushman who can predict the appearance of an eland or an elephant from over the horizon because we still have no way to measure what he does. Only recently, as our recording devices have become more sophisticated—enabling us to hear the long-distance communication of elephants, for instance—have these nomadic people's keenness of observation and their enormous knowledge of the natural world been seen as rivaling or exceeding that of the most experienced field biologist and been given the respect they deserve. But the question remains, How did they learn so much without radio telemetry, time-lapse photography, sensitive microphones—without even a ruler? The answer is hard for us to embrace. Such cultures differ from ours not in their lack of technology but in their immersion in quiet—a quiet that permits them to hear subtler voices than those that come to our ears. They live among more ellipses . . . a state that we consider full of omission and that they see and hear as gravid with information.

Asking lodgepoles to allow themselves to be made into a house before felling them (even standing "dead" ones, for they haven't lost their spirit) is, I guess, my way of living that tradition. Perhaps a better word than "living" would be "hearing"—hearing the spirit of the grand and imposing (these lodgepoles) filter right down into the meek and innocuous, then turning that hearing into action. A few years ago, I began to put vegetable cuttings outside and not solely for the utilitarian end of making compost for my garden. It seemed that the salad scrapings were happier changing state in the grass around my cabin than in a landfill among unacknowledged trash.

"Wow!" say those who haven't watched the body language of the natural world express how it wishes to be treated. "This is far-fetched homage." Maybe . . . maybe. One can also look at the accretion of these small, heartfelt gestures—saying "thank you" to the elk who becomes your winter's meat, bidding good-bye and hello to lodgepoles—as a way of moving through the world (what a Christian might call "soul," a New Age practitioner "aura," and a shaman "spirit"), a way of moving that is the real reason—rather than their stature or skin color—that no one mistakes a Sherpa or a Bushman for an American. The reverence that we enforce in our museums, concert halls, and places of worship these people of less compartmentalized cultures give freely to all their surroundings.

When someone from Western culture gives reverence to all in this way, he or she is often judged as slightly touched, certainly maudlin, not grounded. His or her beliefs, if carried out by many, are seen as leading to economic depression, entropy, the end of society as we know it. Again, that's one way to embrace the world. But a person can admit that everything counts without simultaneously becoming inert. In fact, such an admission can make one more full . . . mindful . . . thoughtful . . . careful . . . which is another way of saying that one grows appreciative of the sacrifices being made to sustain life and that by appreciating them more, one chooses wisely those sacrifices that must be made. Another word for this state of mind is compassion. Not surprisingly, the consumptive age in which we live is uneasy with the state of mind and heart that such words imply. With only so much space on our biggest hard disks, or in our walk-in closets, can any of us make room for a Father in heaven or—closer by and more likely to be trampled by our thoughtlessness—the Mother under our feet?

Taking off my gloves, I touch the bank of swarded earth behind me. For a moment—the bell mare's tinkle floating down the mountainside, the thump of Milo's hooves in the soft undergrowth—I feel her rich beneath us, valleyed and jagged with mountains to be sure, but on the whole curvaceous and breast-smooth, stretching away to the horizons . . . the Earth.

These days, in a return to the animism that informed the cultures that preceded the pagan Greeks and Romans, we have begun to speak to her: Gaia, Doni, Baba Yaga, Sedna, Mother. She has so many names, holdovers and extrapolations from all those peoples who understood paradise as right here in whatever Mosquito Creek they were logging, not above them and not in the future. Myself, I haven't found a name to which I can truly speak, though at times like this, when I have my hands resting upon her understory and put my mouth in her for a taste—leaf, grass, berry, earth—I hear my voice responding to my stomach with the sound nursing mammals make, "Mmmm." At such a moment, I think of her as no more and no less than this sound, "Mmmm." First food, first warmth, first name, first mystery . . . our first and last resting place.

Bearded and slight, his blue eyes laughing, Tonio joins me on the skid trail. We wrap chain around a previously bucked log, then send Milo galumphing through the forest. In another moment, Woody appears with his orange chain saw, which all of us respect but dislike for its noise. He pulls the starter cord and the high-pitched "brrrrr-brrrrr-brrrrr" rips through the forest. Manicuring the path toward the lodgepoles, concerned about the width of the trail needed to get these giant trees out with the two-horse team, he flicks the bar toward the base of a six-foot-high spruce who has had the misfortune to grow too close to the path we have chosen. He decapitates it neatly at ground level, and before it can fall he catches it on the bar while still holding down the trigger. The buzzing chain tosses the sapling aside like a child hit by a car. Without a glance to the spruce, Woody continues to move through the forest, swinging his scythe.

I walk ahead of him, coming at last to the big tree I lingered by. Staring up to where it writes upon the sky, I stretch up an arm and place my palm flat against its trunk. Cone . . . seed . . . tree . . . house.

"Thanks," I say.

Woody comes in, makes a wedge-shaped cut on the downhill side, aiming it for the trail we have cleared. Sawdust flies around his knees like wheat from a thresher. He moves to the opposite side of the trunk and makes the felling cut. For what seems like a moment held in amber—the crouching man, the orange saw, the flying sawdust, the white trunk anchored into a pool of sunlight—the tall lodgepole doesn't move. Then it starts its slow silent arc through the canopy. I mark it: there against the sky; there beginning to sway; there swooshing, whooshing, crashing with a mighty breaking of branches and a dull solid thud, bouncing once before coming to rest. Soil to soil . . . earth to earth . . . our brief and lovely shelter. Standing next to the stump, I look up and see a blue hole where a world just stood.

TROPHIES

This is the hunter's sweetest story: to bring back the unusual and have it remind us of our connection to country. It's what goes beyond the meat—these trophies. They last when the freezer has been emptied, and perhaps they don't have to be horns or antlers. Sometimes they can be nothing more than a single, clear thought, seen like a cairn that changes our direction.

Bob and I drove toward the Oregon Buttes as the big, wide, salmon-colored sprawl of the Wyoming desert opened before us. Pronghorn began to sprint alongside the sandy road. Tan, white, and sleek, they burst from arroyos and galloped toward higher ground. Panting in the heat, they left clouds of dust in the September air. Bucks with fourteen-inch horns sped by like starlings. Here and there, we could spot a fifteen-incher standing sentry on a butte. Taking such an animal could put one's name in the record book.

This, of course, hadn't been my intent when I drove out for the last day of antelope season. I had intended to get a pronghorn for salami and sausage and save the elk for steaks. But the idea of shooting an antelope two minutes after starting and going home to put it through the grinder seemed like no hunt at all. So to stay longer we played the game of those who aren't immediately hungry—we looked harder for the bigger.

We forded a muddy wash and climbed the back of a long ridge; it might have been an enormous wave, curling over with sage. Just where it broke, we stopped. We had to. Had we gone farther, we could have plunged half a thousand feet into the canyons below.

There, among the maze of gray towers, on a knob higher than the rest, stood a wild horse, black as coal, head erect, looking over the country. He could see a long way, as could we—a hundred miles to the horizon, etched here and there by an old surveyor's trail, a faint red line through the pale green sage, beginning nowhere and leading to openness devoid of any destination—and overhead the sky was so enormous and crazy blue it made me catch my breath.

We walked a long circle away from the Isuzu, Bob spotting about three antelope to my one. Once a professional guide, now a builder, he has the sharpest eyes of anyone I know and is inspired to look. In fact, he's one of those rare people who, on foot and without the use of dogs, have actually spied a mountain lion. Thin and tan, with a gentle smile and a balding rim of curly hair, he also loves to hunt, which doesn't necessarily mean shoot. I have seen him carry his rifle in the field for days without loading it.

By chance, he looked one way and I the other, and below us, at the edge of a dry streambed, I saw a buck courting two does. Instantly, I knew this buck was larger than any we had seen; larger, in fact, than any buck antelope I had ever seen in my life. I dropped behind a pile of rocks, and Bob slipped beside me.

From three hundred yards off, we watched the buck circle the does, nudge their rears, and chase them.

"He'll go sixteen," said Bob.

I knew exactly what he meant. Inches. But more. Ever since Rowland Ward, the Boone and Crockett Club, and Safari Club International began to publish their record books, individuals who have applied their competitive streaks to hunting have taken to describing animals by the measurement of their horns and antlers, or the points these measurements produce after being transcribed by a formula. Thus a "185" sheep or a "390" elk puts you well up in the B & C record book, as does a sixteen-inch pronghorn. All of which is understandable—as a people we love numbers. They seem to give us a precise way to measure our accomplishments and help us forget that there aren't exact ways to measure those ambiguous parts of ourselves, like conscience, sympathy, and love.

I looked at my watch. We had been out two hours, which didn't seem long enough. Nevertheless, sixteen-inch antelope don't come along every day. Just as I put the crosshairs on the buck, the does broke from him, galloping off three hundred yards into some willows, and he followed. I was relieved. Now we'd have to stalk him.

We hurried to where a ramp of steep clay led off the ridge. Dropping out of sight, we circled behind some tall eroded fins, like red stalagmites, crawled across a salt pan, and found ourselves in the wash that led directly to the antelope. I plucked some grass, tossed it, and watched it drift sideways from us. Slowly, we began. I knew that within fifteen minutes we'd be in range, and I slowed down. It seemed that we had just started. Placing my feet carefully, I noticed some elk spoor, and I was surprised to see that the big deer were out here in the desert. Stopping to pick up a pellet, I thought of the forested valleys and yellow parks that I hunted in the Gros Ventre country to the north.

The Gros Ventre country. How many days and weeks and months and years had I spent there until the game trails *between* the game trails had become familiar, and I could walk to places by starlight? I had a great sense of patience there, not because I am a very patient man but because I have loved that place more than most. In fact, once, for no other reason than an overwhelming desire to do so, I lay on the sun-warmed grass and put my nose in the earth, inhaling deeply as if the land were a woman. It smelled of chlorophyll, tubers, and roots . . . my roots. I think I have been patient in that country because I like being out in it, a strange turn of phrase that neatly explains being outside one's normal shelter while being immersed in a home. There, out in the country, shooting quickly has seemed dumb, for then being out in it would be over. Last season, I had passed on a four-point elk, then a five-pointer, and even a six-pointer, the last with Bob by my side. He, too, had raised his rifle at the bachelor club of bulls and hadn't fired.

The following week, after sleeping at the trailhead, I walked back to the valley in which we had seen the bulls and which had become familiar over summers and falls. Bob had had to work. As I set off, I saw the print of a grizzly in the frozen mud, an eleven-year-old male who frequented the area. Then I shut off my headlamp and walked by the starlight, listening to the increasing hush of the creek below me.

I was too early, an hour early, which is exactly what I had intended. I sat, drinking tea from a vacuum bottle, until the black sky turned charcoal gray. Then I slipped into the meadow and saw them: fifty cows and a half dozen bulls. Leaving my pack and taking only the rifle, I crawled the last two hundred yards on my belly, then ever so slowly turned into a sitting position in the midst of the elk in the last bit of darkness.

A four-pointer walked within twenty yards of me, stared at me, walked on. The six-point bulls were mixed among the cows and occasionally bugled to one another, their voices turning to steam in the cold. But it was the end of the rut, and their challenges weren't bellicose.

From one to the other of the bulls, I trained my glasses, waiting for the dawn to brighten. How could I choose? I lingered on the largest. Why is larger always better? From the largest I turned away, finding a bull whose antlers were more symmetrical. Perhaps symmetry said more clearly what I felt about this country—its shape of wholeness and peace, and how elk seemed a distillate of the country's water, grass, and air. Whole, clean, solid.

The bull also stood closer than any of the other elk, within fifty paces, so I knew that I could hit him in the neck and drop him instantly. He cropped some grass, and when he looked directly at me, I shot. When the scope returned to where he had been standing, I could see only the tip of one antler sticking toward the dawning sky.

The cows and other bulls looked up, startled, then continued to graze while slowly moving off. I didn't rise until they were out of sight, then walked to the bull and saw that he had been killed so suddenly that he still had grass sticking from his mouth. His right hooves lay in the prints where he had been standing. I touched the smooth ivory tips of his antlers. A six-by-six—six tines to a side, the configuration of the mature bull wapiti.

As I gutted him, a flock of trumpeter swans flew overhead, honking, and another herd of elk, led by another six-by-six, forded the river. He stopped and bugled.

Six-by-six. I felt the antlers again, their rough cornices around the pedicels, the polished tines, this benchmark and symbol of arrival, like a sub-three-hour marathon for the runner, like a twenty-thousand-foot peak for the mountaineer, or a class V rapid for the kayaker. What Aldo Leopold called a *certificate* (his italics), what you bring home, attesting that you've been somewhere and done something, that you've exercised, as he said, "skill, persistence, or discrimination in the age-old feat of overcoming, outwitting, or reducing-to-possession." Except in hunting, the certificate you bring home is dead. No one else can run or climb or boat it. It's not a time on a clock, an eternal mountain, or an endlessly flowing rapid. It is finite, removed from everyone else's enjoyment, particularly its own.

That's why it has seemed important to me to always examine what you're doing out in the country; to be attentive before you send the shot on its way. It's important to believe that you've spent enough time there, watching, listening, intermingling; and to know that what you're doing—killing—is not only imperfect and unclear, but can also be done respectfully only when you remain unsure and somewhat doubtful. Not so doubtful that you won't do it, which would remove you from participating in the great cycles of food gathering and death, but doubtful enough to know that converting animals into food will never be a totally joyous business, that it will always be undercut by a measure of sorrow—one of the basic constituents of the web in which we live and why some of us go back and back. Being out in it isn't the model of what is. It is what is.

From the steep bank of the streambed I could see nothing more than the antelope's horns above the sage, fifteen yards off—about as close as you ever get to a pronghorn. But I could see only his horns. Dropping back, I circled around to come at him from the side. As I crawled along, a short-eared owl flapped from the willows and flew over my head, craning its wise monk's face to look at me—a portent, I thought, a reminder to be cautious.

I eased over the bank, and the three antelope jerked up their heads, black eyes bugging. They leapt up a small hill and ran against the sky full tilt. I put the rifle on the buck, slipped off the safety—ninety yards, offhand, running—and let him go.

"You'll never get a chance like that again," said Bob, walking up to me.

And I didn't. But I got another, almost as good, in some ways better.

We hiked back to the car and made a wide circle across the plains. A herd of wild horses—twenty-five of them with three colts—crossed before us: cinnamon and sorrel creatures with long manes and sweeping tails, who gazed over their shoulders at us with regal curiosity. The sky became a soft and ruffly blue, the hills a wounded red; on a bluff, we spotted a herd of does and one large buck—fifteen inches if he was an inch—overseeing them.

My luck seemed enormous, but somehow it didn't please me. I wanted to camp in this place, spend a few days here, but I didn't have the time. Knowing this, and feeling uneasy, I could have gone home without even trying for the buck. But Bob wanted me to take him. Not that he said it in so many words. It was just the feeling I got from him: This was his spot, and I was his friend. He had been here the weekend before, had camped out, and taken a good antelope—over fourteen inches. Now he wanted me to do the same.

So we stalked up a dry stream, peeked over its top, and saw the herd four hundred yards off.

"Might as well take him," he said.

The antelope seemed too far away. Well, not really. But I was being obstinate and careful. So I crawled through the sage, across a cactus field, over some shale, using every little depression to shield my passage until I was about 120 yards from the pronghorn and had spent forty-five minutes.

Lying on my belly, I watched him through the scope: white and tan, moving among his harem with head high, horns polished, strutting, chasing off young bucks, rounding up straying females.

The setting sun began to flare in the scope, and I waited for the does who shielded him to step aside. Finally, they did, and still I watched him, wondering why I couldn't shoot when I had had no problem with the elk whose antlers now sat on my dresser. I knew as well that within the next month I would shoot again, when the right elk crossed my path.

Suddenly, the antelope stared at me—stared for three long seconds—then wheeled and trotted off, the does and young bucks following him. I stood and watched them go.

Turning around, I saw Bob walk toward me. He looked dejected, binoculars hanging from his hand and a sour expression on his face. It was the last day of antelope season, and now I'd have no chance until the following year.

As he came up to me, I asked, "Are you mad?"

"No," he said. "Why didn't you shoot?"

"Does were in the way."

He looked at me, then quickly began to walk to the car.

I emptied the rifle and followed him, sorry that I hadn't pleased him. He was my friend, and who doesn't like to please his friends? And then I thought of my friends far and wide and what they would have said had I put one in the book. Who doesn't like applause?

Bob reached the car and took a pop from the cooler. I stopped and looked up the long valley where the pronghorn had gone. Still running, they were now well into a canyon, its walls deep in shadow. The rumps of the last three animals were lit like fireflies.

Then they disappeared, and I thought about how next year I'd come back and camp. After you've gone to bed in a piece of country and woken up in it and spent another day walking through it, you may know it well enough to take home a trophy . . . at least the kind that makes you reflect on what you really want to hang on the wall.

WHOSE LAND IS THIS LAND?

Between two basins . . . north slope . . . black timber. The horses' hooves raised puffs of dust in the trickle-down pools of filtered sunlight. In an electric green swale, a moose paused in his feeding and watched us watch him.

It had been a simple wish: break routines, leave the watches behind, ride the high country. And only a few hours out we had already reduced our lives to what we could carry in our panniers, time measured in days and nights—a week of riding—instead of hours.

Somewhere—below, to the left, at the bottom of a steep ravine—ran Cub Creek, almost a sound, the presence of water. Ahead, through the tops of the conifers, a glimpse of bold plateau and sky: puma yellow, faithful blue, the mountains still corniced with snow: Absarokas, Wyoming. Roof of the world . . . heart of home.

We rode toward the sky, rode through the musky trail of horse scent—hay and methane—and the evanescent drift of balsam. So heady, it was like riding through liquor.

The sun sank behind us and pushed us forward toward the Continental Divide—Benj on Whisk; I on Tinker; Gringo, the pack horse, walking free; Merle, the golden Lab, on point, chasing squirrels. Chest-deep in lupine, the color of honey, he looked over his shoulder, panting his laugh and thrashing his tail, saying what everyone was feeling: How good to be moving.

Riding between the long shadows of the trees, we crossed a meadow descending to the creek, found the old hitching post and fire circle left by those who had camped here before us— riders for several hundred summers, those on foot for thousands of years before that. No surprise. The meadow held last sun, caught first light, and had good grass with water nearby.

We stacked the tack and curried the horses, picketing them in the hock-high grass. Starting the stove, setting the pot to boil, we sat on our pads with the saddles for backrests and a bag of nuts between us, our legs stretched out like the first kings, when there were so few people on earth that everyone felt the grace of space surround them.

Then the stars appeared in the deepening blue—one, two, four, the Dipper taking shape. And nothing to do except eat and watch the horses. The sky so clear between the mountain walls, the night so mild, that we lay right where we were, pulling our bags over us, the heaven so dense with stars that the horses appeared like ancient white ghosts grazing on a field of silk.

Not a bad way to spend some reflective time, I thought, in a time when the Grand Old Party, the party of my father and his father before him, had been trying to reshape how all these federal lands through which we were riding—and what many of us have considered public ground, the commons—should be managed. Watching a shooting star, I remembered the warm spring days just past in Washington, D.C., when I had watched the angry floor debate in the House and Senate, more like the Barnum and Bailey Circus that was in town than the supposedly august body known as Congress. I had listened to the scolding the chief of the Forest Service had received from the Senate Energy and Natural Resources Committee for allowing conservation organizations and the courts to dictate his annual cut. The senators felt that he had been remiss in not asking Congress to pass legislation that would make it more difficult for citizens to sue his agency. In the House Appropriations Subcommittee for the Interior, the tone had been more moderate but the intent the same.

From committee to committee and agency to agency, the agenda was clear: streamline the planning process; deregulate; amend the Endangered Species Act so as to minimize court challenges that had stymied development on private lands and resource extraction on public ones. Ideas about selling off federally owned buildings, refuges, and parks also flew around the capital. In short, the evolving Contract with America, created by the Republican Party to reform government after the 1994 midterm election, made one of its goals giving back power to individuals and localities, including power to decide what to do with land.

Some of the contract—overhauling our taxation and welfare systems, making government more accountable, smaller, and less intrusive, and compensating property owners who lose a significant part of their land's value because of environmental restrictions—is welcome. You only have to try to build a house, as I've been doing, to realize the stupidity, waste, and utter unreasonableness of some regulations, such as mandatory installation of radon mitigation devices *before* the house can be closed in and tested for radon. If no radon is present, a thousand dollars has been wasted on labor and materials for a device that can be easily retrofitted. Or take the requirement that smoke detectors must be installed in exactly the near-ceiling locations stipulated by the building code, even though in some parts of a high-ceilinged house this will mean that they cannot be easily serviced, ensuring that the first time they ring a false alarm they will be disconnected. Or consider my county's regulation on septic systems. New homeowners must install a system designed to handle what the county has calculated as the fastest draining ground in its jurisdiction. If your ground happens to drain considerably faster than this base rate (as mine does, which would suggest a less elaborate system), you are still required to install the more extensive (and expensive) equipment, wasting resources, material, and human labor.

Though I've been a lifelong conservationist and supporter of environmental regulations, these inanities made me appreciate the ire of the Sagebrush Rebellion and the so-called Wise Use Movement. However, regulation isn't the culprit. It's regulation that is badly written and inflexibly administered. Unfortunately, being a reactive lot, we humans tend to overfix or sweep away what needs modification and tinkering, and that's what's happening now.

Some of this "fixing" has serious and potentially unfriendly consequences for wildlife, ranging from the clearly awful—such as scrapping the Endangered Species Act and suspending protective fish and wildlife laws to expedite salvage logging in the national forests under the smoke screen of "fire protection"—to the possibly damaging, such as President Clinton offering the states management of 2.2 million acres of federal Waterfowl Production Areas, bought with duck-stamp money. Such moves are only the tip of the iceberg. On Capitol Hill and in conservative think tanks such as the Heritage Foundation, some are talking seriously about selling our national lands.

In the morning we rode up a basin of subalpine grass, which

merged into the high tundra at twelve thousand feet. The distant mountains spired the horizon, and the Continental Divide stretched before us, great waves of undulating land cobbled with the gray rocks of ancient volcanoes. On north-facing slopes, the snowdrifts lay deep and tinged with pink, their odd shade caused by névéphilic algae the color of roses.

Below us lay five national forests, two national parks, two national wildlife refuges—all the country of Yellowstone and the nation's first national forest and park—as if viewed from an airplane, except it was moving by in stately, horse-paced time, giving us an opportunity to scout what we had come to see. Around us, within a hundred yards, herds of elk relaxed on the crescents of pink snow—cows with frisky calves and bulls in velvet. Here and there, boulders had been uprooted, the ground around them excavated as if a fleet of backhoes had been at work. They had. The country's grizzlies had been digging ground squirrels. A pair of golden eagles soared on thermals, and red-tailed hawks dipped lower, skimming the tundra. Looking ahead, we searched for bighorns.

In the late afternoon, we turned the horses loose. Nearly sitting on their tails, they found their own way down a steep scree slope and into a basin lush with grass and running with a freshet. On the topographic map, the drainage was unnamed, but, geographically speaking, it was the east fork of the south fork of the Buffalo. An unwieldy name if there ever was one. So we called it Tinker's Basin, after the horse who had led us down.

The evening was so mild that we didn't bother with the tent. Sitting on the grass by our panniers, we ate dinner and watched the moon rise over the divide, its full gold disc skating over the peaks. It was so quiet you could hear the horses rip grass from the earth.

Of all the many positive attributes of the preindustrial world—space, quiet, clean air, and potable water—this kind of quiet has been disappearing the fastest. Its balm has vanished from the secluded parks that once provided privacy in urban places. It has almost disappeared from rural landscapes, which once surrounded cities and are now interconnected suburbs. And it's no longer one of the defining attributes of our national parks and nonwilderness, multiple-use public lands, where timber production, fossil-fuel extraction, mining, and motorized recreation share the turf. In fact, the only place you can find such quiet is in the roadless backcountry. Its possible elimination would be a major, twofold loss: Such quiet country is synonymous with intact, healthy wildlife habitat; and it's also the place in which many of us find sustenance for our souls. They are the nation's sacred places, akin to houses of worship.

For the latter reason, Congress passed the Wilderness Act of 1964. For the former, fish and game departments continue to set aside critical habitat, especially winter range, where wildlife is not to be disturbed by mechanized vehicles.

Of course, a few ATVs in all of Nevada or a few snow machines in all of Wyoming won't threaten the big banks of quiet—unless, that is, one goes by you when you're in the middle of talking with God or, more prosaically, stalking an elk. However, when mechanized vehicles number in the thousands and people in the tens of thousands, as they do in some of our national forests, not only does each individual's experience deteriorate, but wildlife becomes stressed. Scale—the cumulative effect of many individuals or the more massive effects of industry—matters. It matters enormously.

Today, about 90 percent of the United States has roads, most of our rivers are dammed, and nearly all of our wetlands in some regions have been filled. Given the scale of how we've changed nature, do we want to transform the remaining small slice of the unaltered continental pie—the remnant "wildernesses" such as Benj and I have been riding through—into what the other 90 percent looks and sounds like? This isn't merely an aesthetic question but a wildlife one. Put roads into unroaded country and you sign a warrant of ill health or even death for numerous species.

The following day found us on the Buffalo Plateau, straddling the headwaters of the continent. Far below and to our right, the Shoshone River flowed toward the Atlantic. To the west, the Snake curved toward the Pacific.

In twenty miles of riding, we saw not another person, and at sunset we dropped into the south fork of the Yellowstone River. Waterfalls like white mare's tails fell hundreds of feet to the valley floor. Leaving the trail behind, we rode deep into an amphitheater of tall grass. Above us, on the rim of the canyon, tiny pines were silhouetted against the violet sky. We hobbled the horses, built a fire, and sat listening to the river flow, its hush giving no indication as to what century or millennium we were riding through. Elk had left their hoofprints in the river gravel, and we decided that this would be our hunting valley for the fall. Then, the moon rose over the divide, turning the waterfalls into silver plumes. You could have thought, sitting by that fire in the silence of the world, that the forest and rivers went on forever.

Of course, they don't, which makes it imperative that those who act as their stewards be both competent and well intentioned.

For better and for worse (and we've had both for nearly a century), the federal government has been the steward of such lands

in the shape of its agencies: the Forest Service, the Bureau of
Land Management, the Fish and Wildlife Service, the National
Marine Fisheries Service, and the Environmental Protection
Agency. These bureaucracies can be thought of as the referees of
the commons, their charge being the health of people, wildlife,
land, water, and air in those landscapes where no property rights
exist and hence the temptation is large for each individual to use
the commons for his short-term benefit while depreciating their
value for the many.

Some free-market champions claim that if we sell off these
lands—"privatize" them and create defined property rights—we
can improve their stewardship (since people care about their
property) while simultaneously cutting the federal budget. The
second premise, reducing governmental overhead, is probably true
(though states will then have to bear some of the fiscal burdens
the federal government now shoulders). The first, better stewardship because of well-defined property rights, bears scrutiny.

Individual property owners—conservation-minded ranchers,
loggers, hunters, anglers, or just plain old landowners—do often
make the best stewards. Their self-interest and attachment to
wildlife is high, and they live with the consequences of their actions. It would take a leap of faith, however, to believe that these
people will buy national forests, parks, and refuges if they go up
for sale. As the political rhetoric would have us believe that we
are still a nation of family farmers, so too would it have us believe that individual property owners will become the beneficia-
ries of a national lands sell-off. This will not happen. As in the
agribusiness industry, corporations will dominate the field. And
the difference between an individual and a corporation is not
only one of scale but of values.

Corporations, whose interests lie in accumulating capital and increasing profits so as to give investors a high return on their investment, do not have the same interest in land as individuals do. Nor do corporations live with the consequences of their actions to the same extent that individuals do. The individual, family, or community not only has a fiscal investment in a parcel of land but also an emotional one. Individuals nurture land not only because they live directly with the results of their actions but because they also receive returns from their land other than money.

Consider this one example out of many: Huge areas of North America's boreal forest, mostly aspen, are now being cut for pulp, which is then turned into paper. The paper you are now holding in your hands may very well have come from one of these giant clear-cuts and from a seventy-five-year-old tree, which is old for an aspen. However, as debarking techniques have improved, the logging industry has been able to utilize thirty-year-old aspens for pulp manufacture. Growing and cutting such young trees is literally "mowing" a forest, which can no longer, with any accuracy, be called a "forest," complete with old and young trees, decaying matter, and diverse wildlife. It has become a pasture.

Here's the rub. For global corporations interested in supplying pulp to paper factories, it makes no difference whether aspens are forests or pastures. In fact, forests hinder production and thus profits when compared to a pasture. However, if you are a warbler, a caribou, a lynx, a bear, a person who lives and traps in that country, or a visiting wildlife photographer, hunter, or angler, it makes a great deal of difference to you whether you have a forest or a pasture.

Unfortunately, for wildlife and for people who like wildlife, if producing paper from pastures pays better than producing caribou and lynx from forests, it will be profit that dictates what the country looks like. This is how the market works. And it may well be that most of us prefer disposable plates and cups to caribou and lynx. Such is the nature of democracy and capitalism: They don't always produce healthy or fair results. In fact, the U.S. Constitution went out of its way to spell out rights—such as freedom of speech and religion and the right to bear arms—that the majority might someday want to eliminate and which the minority might want to hang on to.

Selling off our great public spaces may become a majority decision of the U.S. populace, but it will mean turning *everyone's* land—your land, my land, about whose fate we can at least vote—into *private* land over which we will have much less say. In the process, the average person will be disenfranchised from the type of democratic hiking, hunting, and angling (that is, access) that we now enjoy, making them the pastimes of the wealthy.

"Hold on there," replies the free-market wisdom, "consumers will have a say about how land is managed through their buying power." True, consumers can express their wishes through their wallets. But national or global markets are not nearly as sensitive as local ones. If your local butcher replaces beef with rattlesnake meat, he will hear about it within a day. When Coca-Cola decided to change the flavor of its renowned drink, it took enormous consumer pressure to reverse corporate policy.

Sadly, wildlife doesn't have nearly the popular following of soft drinks. The majority of us—who don't travel much beyond the end of the road and don't have much investment in wildlife—may allow the public lands of America to become theme parks with fences, gates, and no-trespassing signs. Hunters and anglers—who may be part of the conservative majority but who are in the minority on the issue of wildlife conservation—need to listen to their favorite spot of quiet and come back making some noise to those whom they elected.

There is a difference between reforming how federal agencies—the referees of the commons—operate and getting rid of them entirely. Throwing our public lands open to development or actually selling them off won't be good for quiet, and it won't be good for wildlife.

The point to remember is that the privatization of public lands is not just a battle of the 1990s. It is an ancient and ongoing one. In Europe, from the 1100s on, the commons were enclosed, and access to wildlife and to open country disappeared for the average person and has not yet returned. In the United States, this battle has been fought several times in the twentieth century, most recently during the Sagebrush Rebellion. If public land remains public in North America, the battle over its ownership will no doubt resurface in another generation. When it does, we need to be clearheaded. As we wouldn't sell our rights of free speech, assembly, and worship, neither should we sell our right to wander freely over what is still a free land.

LAST DAY

From the front seat of the car, Merle, my golden Lab, studies the mud-paved, slushy road with a look of concern. We're grinding upward in low four-wheel drive . . . finessing the curves . . . barely holding on. To the left, it's a long way down to the creek, lost in mist; to the right, the conifers rise steeply into the clouds. The last vehicle tracks stopped a mile back, where the pickup of two orange-coated hunters fishtailed into a wide place on the road. Soon the silence grows deeper as the sleet turns to snow, and the slush to a wide, clean cut through the forest.

At eight thousand feet we can go no farther. Where the road becomes a trail, we park. As I load my rifle, Merle leaps into the air and rolls in the snow, overjoyed to be out of the car and trusting to his own four legs.

"Now stay close," I say. He comes to my left side, brows furrowed, mouth closed, all his horseplay gone—Merle the stalker.

The trail climbs slightly, bending around several small, steep ravines, and I can feel my legs protesting. I've been following elk all week and rose at three-thirty this morning. Even a midday nap hasn't taken away the tiredness from seven miles of hiking and my disappointment at finding no elk and no sign of one in my traditional "without fail" spots. But the trail we're now following is an old one, walked many times, so I don't have to think about my direction, and it's also the last day of elk season, which means that, tired or not, I want to watch the sunset.

Not that elk season won't continue for another month. Rather, it's the last day of elk season in my familiar drainages, the country just behind the cabin, where I've taken most of my elk, and where I hike and mountain bike and fish during the summer. It also happens to be the only day that I've hunted this, my favorite trail.

Gaining an old clear-cut and walking through its snowy, silent parks, I reflect on how I let this happen. First there was antelope season and the drive to the Red Desert, our camp in the wash, the glassing (watching with binoculars) from the eroded buttes, and the several stalks that ended with seeing no more than white rumps fleeing. At sundown on our way home, I spotted a buck who was more trusting or, as I've come to see these things, more giving. He let me stalk to within two hundred yards, and it's his sausage that is now moving me up through the Gros Ventre mountains.

And then there was the bighorn, which this year evoked my hots for altitude and hard climbing. Here in Wyoming, sheep hunting is called "the once-in-a-lifetime experience" because it takes so long to draw a permit (some unlucky people never do), and once you've been selected in the computer lottery, you can't apply again for another five years. But such details never fazed me. I drew my tag in only four years and, having scouted diligently in August and having seen nearly a dozen legal rams, I knew that I'd be packing out sheep horns and eating ram steaks on opening day.

The saddest part of hubris is that the individual afflicted with it can never see that's he's grown full of himself. I went in with my llamas, deep into the Absarokas, that great high plateau and gorge country east of Yellowstone. And the night before opening day, it snowed, snowed so much that I didn't see a single ram in those high alpine basins, now desolate and drifted over. I hunted a week, found nothing but ewes and lambs, came home, regrouped, went back, hunted in the trees, climbed into steep hanging valleys that few people ever venture into, while glassing for hours . . . days. And I didn't see a single legal ram. Not one. In the meantime, elk season was going by . . . and is now nearly gone, at least in the country I like the best.

Merle and I go around the giant fallen Douglas fir, which as you return in the dark lets you know that you've come halfway to the roadhead. Then we gingerly cross the swampy meadow whose suck lets you know that you're approaching the downed tree. Finally, we climb a sage slope that leads to the knoll with the grand view. Squall lines of snow blow from the Tetons; bruised yellow clouds roil where the hidden sun has begun to set; and in a moment of clearing, I can see our cabins and yurts, far, far away in the valley. A moment later the village is snatched away by the clouds.

But the cold air has rejuvenated me. My mind clears and the loggedness slips from my legs. In another moment, I feel memories blowing on the wind. Looking across the steep ravine before me, I remember the five-by-five elk that I stalked and found on Halloween six years ago. Over the next ridge, I shot the cow of '90, and just uphill from her, the five-pointer of '91, whom Merle pointed to, tail lashing, before either of us saw him. And how many wapiti have I seen in these high drainages and not shot at? Surely, in the next hidden park, I'll find another.

We turn into the forest, following the ridge crest and looking down its steep north face into the black timber. We go across a wide, willowy meadow where I've watched moose sparring and up through another stand of thick conifers before reaching the parks that saddle the ridge between the middle and south forks.

The light has grown dim; tiny flakes fall from the leaden sky; Merle and I stand on the edge of a meadow and listen. We haven't seen a single sign of large life except the tracks of moose, but a powerful presence now comes through the air. Darting among the trees, the movement turns our heads. Gray and immense, the shadow grows wings and lights in a snag fifty yards off. Fully three feet tall, the great gray owl stares at us. When I raise my binoculars, I see his enormous yellow eyes peering at me. He weaves his head back and forth, getting our range, then with a silence made more inspiring by his size, flaps toward us. Twenty feet out, he veers, cranes his head, and arcs back into the forest—a wonderful sign, filling the afternoon with mystery and clarity.

Up we continue, the dog and I, now so used to each other that we seem to move as one . . . steadily up, passing squirrel tracks and rabbit tracks, the dumbbell-shaped prints of weasels, and the beautiful feathered striations of a raven's wings, showing where it momentarily landed. But there's not an elk track to be seen. Still, we go on, aiming for the peak that looks over the south fork, and from where, on a clear day, one can see all the mountain ranges of northwestern Wyoming and southern Montana. One can also look down into several high, hidden basins, and from there I've comfortably watched elk as they traversed from one drainage to another, especially at dusk. When all the other spots have failed, this overlook has brought me to them.

We turn downward into a marshy swale, avoiding a section of windblown timber, and follow a moose run into the forest, which has grown dark. Then the long trudge through shin-deep snow to the final ridge crest. Keeping behind the rimrock's fringe of trees, I sweep the basins below with my glasses, but nothing moves. The high country has really gone to winter.

The last quarter mile to the top seems to take an hour. In reality, it takes but a few minutes, and when Merle and I reach the summit, with its the trees heeled over from the nearly perpetual wind, we find nothing. It is the very last of shooting light, the magic hour of the dusk, and there's nothing but vapor. The uplifted clouds fume over our perch; the Tetons have disappeared; even our trail of foot- and paw prints vanishes fifty yards behind us.

How satisfying it would have been to have stalked an elk in this wonderful corner of my world, to have gone out in the last few hours of the season and done what I've often done before: felt the presence of wapiti and found them. But not today. I stare into the clouds and feel the pang inside, not for the elk I might have gotten and didn't, but for the other reason that I came up here, and which, until now, I have put aside.

I pick up a handful of snow and throw some to the north, then to the east, and to the south, and finally to the west, lingering in each direction while I think of my father, who is about to have surgery to remove a lung. I take a deep breath of cold and snow and pine, feeling the sweet Wyoming air go down into me, which is really my father in a younger guise. And I think of him in my mind, as well as through my feet, asking the country upon which I'm standing and the winds of the sky to give him and the entire family strength in this mortal time. I rub some snow on my face, his face, the being to whom he helped give life and who has had the good fortune to push so close to the sky. Then I remember his encouragement, his gentle suggestion to do one's best, which has carried me into these high places on the last days of many a fall. All this Merle watches somberly, his fur blown by the wind. It's not the first time he's watched me do strange things in the mountains.

I rub some snow on his muzzle, which he licks off, giving his tail a tentative wag.

"Are you ready, big dog?"

He cocks his head and watches me as I unload the rifle, storing the cartridges in my pack, an almost sure sign that we're done hunting and he'll have leave to roam. When I toss the pack on my back and say, "Let's go," he leaps into the air and leads me down into the dark.

A STORY of HOME

No matter how many times I've done the drive, I'm always amazed at the distance: the run up the front range of Colorado, through the red, striated hills, and out onto the plains of Wyoming, the road bending around the Snowy Range and the Medicine Bow, and into the badlands, the Red Desert, the country so big that it seems to crawl by, even at seventy-five miles per hour. Then the approach of the Wind River Mountains, an entire horizon of peaks dusted with snow, going along for a hundred miles by the right side of the car, basin and range, basin and range, until the suddenness of purple willow and conifers marks the beginning of the north country—Hoback Canyon skiffed with snow, like a gate into another world.

The road climbed and climbed, I turned up the Snake, and in the twilight Jackson went by as a two-mile-long flash of car dealers and restaurants, the town square with its four arches of elk antlers desolate under a driving rain. Then I was up in the park, the clouds almost on the road, the Tetons hidden but there, vibrating, looming as the smaller road took me along the cottonwoods, through the sage, and onto a smaller road, and a still smaller one, its craters turned to a lake of mud and water as the rain and big wet snowflakes beat down, mixing fall and winter and welcoming me home.

Shutting off the car, I sat, staring at the woodpile and feeling the tarmac still humming in my head.

"Why don't you really admit why you hunt," said the curly-haired woman in the back row of the meeting room after I was done reading. "It's not all that sensitive shit about being out there and the smells. You just want to kill. I've talked to hundreds of hunters, and they all say that they get off on the killing. Admit it."

She had come with her agenda, as had her two male companions. The one in military fatigues now chimed in, "Why do you use a gun? Why don't you use a knife like the hunter-gatherers you talk about? That would really make you a manly man."

I had thought: Did they listen to what I had read? And before I could say it a big man in the audience turned around and yelled, "Did you even listen to what he said? Why don't you shut up?"

Before someone threw a punch, the woman who officiated at the university reading shut down the question-and-answer period. Signing books, talking to a circle of hangers-on, I looked up to see the third animal rightist standing by the podium—a blue-jean jacket, black long hair, long as mine.

"I appreciate that you've thought about these things deeply," he said, "though you'll never convince me." He lifted a basketball sneaker to show me that he was pure and didn't use leather. Just as he pointed to his rubber soles, the curly-haired woman sidled up, scooped an open pack of Camels from his vest pocket, and left to light up. I wanted to ask her if she knew that the tobacco industry was one of the worst killers of wildlife.

But I said nothing. I don't think that she could have agreed to disagree. She had her world, and I had mine, each with its own internal logic, its story of how things ought to be.

After the faculty dinner and visiting old friends and drinking the good Boulder coffee, like nothing you can get in Wyoming (and we "the Cowboy State"), I drove away from where I had spent three years of my life getting a degree, drove away north and west and north again, feeling the city and the disconnected-from-the-land feeling that pushed me from Colorado years ago falling away one more time.

When I woke, the coals still glowed in the fire and it was snowing, the world incandescent under the clouds. I waxed my boots. I put my knife and saw in my pack, along with a quart of water and a pemmican bar, extra clothes. Soon a red Honda appeared out of the falling snow at the end of the road, and Benj and Scott, two of my hunting partners, started loading their gear in my Subaru, because I was the only one who had put on his snow tires.

As we bounced on the potholed road, Scott, lean and fair, and Benj, round and with graying hair, talked about what they were shooting this year—respectively 180-grain bullets in a .30-06 and 140-grain ones in a .270. Merle, my golden Lab—streamers of blaze orange hanging from his collar—looked at Scott and then at Benj as if following their argument.

We passed Lee, the postman, and his fourteen-year-old son, Lucas, loading their Suburban with cased rifles. We passed Steve, the house mover, in his pickup, a .270 across its back window and a six-by-six elk rack sticking from its bed. We passed Mabel's cabin. In her nineties, she still went out each year for deer and a couple of seasons ago had shot a moose. As we passed Betty's general store, we saw the gruff shop owner, in her late sixties or early seventies, step outside wearing blaze orange. The village was

still one of those places where a person carrying a rifle provoked
about as much comment as a person pushing a lawn mower, and
I thought about how a map of the nation could be drawn that
was not keyed to states or ecological zones but colored by the
music people listened to as they engaged in the tasks of fall: the
thwack of a splitting maul, the pop of distant gunfire, the rasp
of a meat saw.

We parked in a canyon of red rock, where a side valley opened
into an alpine basin, hidden in clouds. Loading the rifles, we
headed up, separating where the forks of two drainages met, Benj
and Scott going east and Merle and I west. The snow continued
to fall heavily, now drier with another 1,500 feet of altitude, occasionally slanting from the southwest, out of which the wind
blew. Intermittently, the long horizontal strata of the mountains
across the valley appeared out of the clouds.

Two days ago, it was summer; now it was the beginning of
winter, just like that, which was just fine. Climbing steadily, the
snow already knee-deep in places but still unconsolidated, I
thought about how five hundred miles moved you from one
logic—shorts and T-shirts and cappuccinos at a sidewalk café—
to another: snow and the migration of ice-age animals. But today
not an elk track marred the snow. It would take a bigger storm
than this to move them down from the ridge tops.

Merle and I went higher, slipping on hidden boulders, trip-
ping over sage, the miles dropping behind. Just before entering
the cloud cover, we stopped to glass across the valley, watching,
listening, smelling. We saw nothing, nothing but the wind made
visible by the slanting of the snow, and nothing but the ghosts it
carried.

Merle and I walking in the gilded light of the aspen last fall, the
doe stopping in a splash of sunlight. Sinking to the ground, talk-

ing to her, I had taken a steady rest, though the shot was only forty-five yards. There seemed to be all the time in the world. I carried her out on my back, down the steep hillside of aspen and pines, through the sage, along the rocky shore of the river, among another grove of pines, and down the canyon, smelling her scent all the time—the musky hide, the cool fresh meat—and feeling her wild weight pressing on my shoulders, a gift from beyond the neat highways of farms and grocers and cash, where all the deaths are hidden. She pressed me down and lifted me up, reminding of what it once took to stay alive.

And then Thanksgiving, the Milky Way so bright that we walked up the frozen creek without using our headlamps. At 7 A.M., at twenty-five below, the snow began to turn into a grayish wash filled with the dark splotches of elk, their breaths fuming at the edge of the pines. Benj and I crawled through the deep powder and waited but couldn't get close enough. The elk drifted one by one, then all together back into the forest, like a brown school of fish. The following mornings were all ten, fifteen below zero, the short days unraveling in snow and cold while the orange light of the woodstove played through its glass door, as I had many cups of tea, until one evening from this knoll I spotted a herd of cows seeping from the timber.

With perhaps twenty minutes of dusk left, Merle and I slid into a draw, ran through the thick forest of two intervening valleys, crept out of the pines, and saw a single elk against the indigo sky with the full moon rising by her side.

I laid my pack in the snow and lay behind it, breathing softly so as not to fog the scope, and said the words of apology to her that may not do anything more than wrap us in our myth, wrapping the deaths we own and the gifts we receive in love and care.

The smack of the bullet hitting and the elk's fall came together. Later, as I gutted her, her herd mates called from the forest, asking her to get up and come with them, which tells a person pretty clearly the cost of turning big social animals like elk into your food.

The next day, Scott and Benj and their wives, April and Janet, helped me drag the elk out on a sled. And Tessa, at that point inside April, started her life eating that elk, whose jerky fed me across the miles of Yellowstone that winter, whose meat helped to feed the rest of my family into the following summer, whose grown calf was now probably in this valley, scenting the air.

I looked into the clouds.

We shared some pemmican, the dog and I, the dog whose mind I could read and who knew how to read mine as well.

"Ready?" I looked into his deep brown eyes under their golden brows.

He leaped up, putting his paws on my shoulders, and licked my face: ready.

We climbed a little more and contoured around a ridge that fell steeply to our left. To our right lay a broad basin of sage, aspen, and conifers. Looking down, I noticed that we had begun to walk in deer tracks.

We turned into the wind that had been blowing across our line of travel. Sifting downhill, knee- then thigh-deep in the snow, we dropped into a sheltered vale where the aspens leaned together like whispering penitents. Uphill, spruce and firs loomed, occasionally one of their branches breaking under its load of heavy snow with the sound of a shot.

I can't say how long we sifted along in that timeless time when motion becomes stillness and stillness drifts slower than smell. When thought disappears and you become present, turning on instinct . . . pausing because of a feeling in your bones. Across a small park, by a stand of pines, gray against green, drifted three deer, coming to a stop as we did. Ears up, antlers shining dead-leaf gold through the falling snow, throat patches grayer than the clouds that surrounded us, they watched.

I sank into the snow, knowing my mouth was talking to them though I made no sound and feeling Merle sink down into the snow behind me, all of us living in that moment when gesture is everything.

They stood broadside to us, heads turned, the smallest of the three deer shielding the two bucks behind him. I knelt, wrapping my arm in the rifle's sling, and thought about the largest buck, whose only vital area exposed was a portion of his neck. The medium-sized buck stood slightly ahead of the smallest deer, his forequarters visible.

Why him, I thought, and not the largest or the smallest? Why him and not me? Why him and not my dog? Since childhood these questions have swirled in my mind, making me put away my guns for a time to think about the questions more clearly. And it's not only that deer and elk taste good that has sent me out again, because I've eaten lentils in curry that taste as fine as any deer or elk. It's much more an answer that concerns participation: to hunt, to fish, to grow some of my own food; to be part of how country lives—birthing, dying, foreclosing one life so another may go on; to acknowledge killing without malice but with intent; to embrace the process still carrying us all along.

Not that I thought all this as I looked at the deer. All that existed in the snow, in the wind, in the approaching dusk, was our breathing in the breath of the country, like being in the arms of the sweetest marriage, full of fun and laughter and impossible sorrow, full of that old unanswerable paradox, that sad refrain: Why this life now and not another?

To the deer I had chosen, I said I was sorry and said it again and said it yet again before hearing the shot. The three bucks bounded away, brownish-gray wraiths amid puffs of snow. Given the distance (short) and my position (solid), it did not seem possible that three deer departed. I unchambered the empty cartridge, put another one in its place, and walked across the small park, asking the powers that move in these mountains to have at least allowed me to miss completely. Perhaps, I thought, the scope had gone out.

The snow was painted with blood. We followed it through the bounding, plowed-out trail, the spray of crimson increasing like the first abstraction of life's unwinding, the snow falling and the clouds low, the dusk now truly upon us. Just over a small rise, one tine shone.

I put down the rifle, knelt by his head, and touched the miracle of his antlers, putting my hand on his warm, swelled neck. His eye was bright and looked at the sky. I picked up one of his svelte hooves that had flown him so long through the forest. Somberly, Merle sat on the opposite side of the buck as we watched his soul fly away. Then the wind came over the mountains and carried away this story of home.

A TALK ABOUT ETHICS

In America, and in general, we dislike hunters. We dislike them because they use tools of destruction. And we dislike them because they kill beings who win our affections—mammals rather than fish. Even those who want to engage primal values often dislike hunters because hunters insist on getting blood on their hands whereas most of us are satisfied with less graphic measures—songs, drums, a simple walk through the trees. Most important, though, we dislike hunters for their dishonesty, for how their actions do not live up to their claims that hunting is a noble and conscientious activity.

Some hunter advocacy groups claim that these accusations are no more than perceptual problems, rooted in animal-rights rhetoric and in urban people's diminished connections to firearms as useful tools, to land and animals, and to natural cycles. Such arguments have a shade of validity as well as a great deal of smoke behind which they conceal the truth: The hunting community has denied the character of many of its members and until very recently has refused to address—deeply, committedly, and spiritually—what constitutes appropriate behavior toward animals.

This denial is no longer being tolerated, just the way our nation, in fits and starts, will no longer tolerate racism, the actions of the alcoholic behind the wheel, abuse within the home, or the unsustainable use of the commons. Intolerance of the hunting community comes about not only because trophy hunters make headlines for violations of the Endangered Species Act, or hunters in the pay of sporting-goods manufacturers are convicted of shooting elk in Yellowstone National Park while making hunting videos. Rather, it is how, on a thousand days in a thousand ways, we witness the people Steven Kellert has called the "dominionistic/sport hunters" act with a callousness that debases everything hunters say about hunting being a sacred connection to our Paleolithic roots.

Kellert's 1978 survey sampled hunters across the nation and found that nearly 40 percent were what he termed the "dominionistic/sport hunter." Often living in cities, these hunters savored competition with and mastery over animals in a sporting contest. "Utilitarian/meat hunters"—those interested in harvesting meat much as they would a crop of wheat—made up 43.8 percent of the sample. The remaining 17.8 percent Keller called "nature hunters." The youngest segment of the hunting population, these individuals knew the most about wildlife, and their goal was to be intensely involved in nature through hunting.

Unfortunately, it has been dominionistic/sport hunters, even though they represent less than 40 percent of America's hunters, who have often set the image for the rest of the hunting community. Despite hunters' best efforts at educating the public about the hunter's role in conserving habitat and species, it is this group's behavior that the public remembers when they hear the word "hunting." Not only are this group's actions highly visible, but as a group they may very well represent more of America's hunters than Kellert's study leads us to believe.

Indeed, they may represent a great many nonhunters. The developer who fills a wetland, homeowners who spread toxic herbicides on their lawns, every one of us who supports monoculture forests, agribusiness, and factory farms participates in a type of dominionistic mastery over wildlife and nature. Often, because the effects of such practices occur far from our daily lives and in the form of what economists call "externalities"—birds, small mammals, and reptiles gobbled up by combines and poisoned as nontarget casualties of pesticides—we overlook the enormous destruction. On the other hand, the dominionistic hunter's actions are visible, premeditated, and often discomforting; they are, however, in keeping with the fundamental beliefs of the culture that has bred him. When hunters' worst colors show, they can easily become our scapegoats and ones that, like oft-reprimanded children, seem to revel in ever more unruly behavior.

As a committed hunter, I say this with regret. I say this with embarrassment. And I say this with frustration. Whereas the hunter was once the teacher and shaman of his culture, he is now the boor. And I'm forced to emphasize this point because on so many days in the field I myself have seen the average hunter bend the rules of fair chase and even the laws of the land—spotting game from aircraft, chasing animals with vehicles, or shooting on the evening before the season opens. On so many occasions, such dubiously taken animals end up in the record books, our record-keeping organizations paying only lip service to the standards that they have set. I have seen downed hen mallards left to float away so they wouldn't be included in the day's bag limit, and hunters retrieve them only grudgingly when their obvious disregard has been pointed out. Some of my own neighbors have taken bucks on their girlfriends' tags; around my home, two mule deer, an elk, three antelope, and a black bear with triplets have been poached during the last few years; several coyotes have been hung on a fence to rot because they were, well, "just coyotes"; and, most recently, one of Yellowstone's reintroduced wolves was shot because it was "just a wolf." But these aren't the real hunters, goes the hunting community's old saw, these are the lawbreakers, these are the people who indulge in inappropriate behavior.

On the contrary, I believe that these individuals *are* hunters and that their attitudes are founded in the same values that Americans have held about the commons—namely, take as much as you can before it's used up. For a century and a half, starting slowly with the writings of Henry David Thoreau and gathering speed with the forest and park campaigns of John Muir, the American conservation movement has tried to alter the consciousness of "use-it-up-and-move-on." For hunting, this change in consciousness was initiated by Theodore Roosevelt in 1887 with his founding of the Boone and Crockett Club. Their invention of the idea of "fair chase" only began to create a genuine hunting ethic, the rough design for what Aldo Leopold would later call "the land ethic," and what I'm calling here appropriate and compassionate behavior toward nature.

However, a hundred years after Roosevelt transformed the nation's leading hunters into some of its most effective conservationists, the most compelling ideas about our evolving relationship with animals often come not from hunters but from nonhunters and even antihunters. Indeed, the story of the modern hunter as the best of conservationists often seems, at least to this hunter, like an exhausted myth.

In part, this myth says that it is hunters who are active and fit and who know nature and wildlife best. However, if you visit the forests during hunting season, you find the roads full and the backcountry largely empty, many hunters "camped" in RVs full of amenities. When hunters are asked to support the creation of legally designated wilderness areas in which hardy recreation takes place (and which often are, one might add, irreplaceable wildlife habitat), they often choose to side with the so-called Wise Use Movement and others who want to build roads through the last remaining wild country.

The old hunting myth goes on to say that the hunter is a disciplined, reluctant taker of life. Yet if this were the case, why are so many of my nonhunting neighbors afraid to go into the woods during hunting season? Perhaps it's because there are too many hunters who resemble the fellow I met several years ago on a trail. I asked how he had done. He replied that he hadn't seen any elk but that he had taken "a sound shot." When I asked what a "sound shot" was, he replied, "Oh, you know, I heard something in the timber and shot at it." His disregard for the suffering—animal or human—that he might have caused was borne out a few years later when, not far from my house, one elk hunter shot and killed his good friend when the friend bugled.

The myth goes on to say that hunting is a courageous and sometimes dangerous activity. The sporting press has been particularly fond of painting this picture. However, with the advent of nature documentaries and adventure travel, millions of people have witnessed the behavior of wildlife who are not being threatened. After you have fished fifty feet from several brown bears in Alaska and come to no harm, it is difficult to believe that shooting one is either a courageous or dangerous activity.

The myth goes on to say that hunters hunt to return to a world of origins, simplicity, and honest interaction with nature.

But when you look at hunters, especially bow hunters, in the pages of sporting magazines, in the equipment catalogs, and in the woods, they look like a cross between Darth Vader and Rambo. If you go to one of the annual trade shows that display new outdoor equipment, a hundred people a day will try to sell you a new hearing aid, a new camouflage pattern, a new scent, cartridge, or bow that will improve your chances of getting game, and too few hunters question the replacement of skill and intuition by gadgets.

Of course, using improved technology to enhance survival has been one of the hallmarks of our species since ancient times. Does this inventive tradition mean that we are permitted no room to discriminate between laser sights and atlatls? Developing codes that distinguish appropriate from inappropriate technology is one of the challenges hunters need to face and have not.

All these examples show the discrepancy between who hunters claim to be and who their actions demonstrate that they are. Many outdoor people, including backpackers, canoeists, climbers, and skiers, have noticed that hunters haven't cornered the market on nature lore, woods savvy, or hardihood. In fact, they are frequently lacking in them.

Actions also speak louder than words when it comes to the hunter's relationship with the animals he or she kills. When the hunting community, believing that it can't relinquish any form of what it calls "hunting," refuses to denounce such activities as shooting live animals for target practice or for competition, its moral stature vanishes.

The image of the hunter as a farseeing conservationist also comes into question when hunters and the agencies that represent them refuse to consider the idea that some wild species, not typically eaten as food, might no longer be hunted for sport. These would include brown bears, wolves, and coyotes. Some hunters tend to reject such proposals as radical thinking, yet they are increasingly being floated by hunters themselves. Indeed, they evolved out of the ideas of some farseeing hunters at the end of the nineteenth century who suggested that certain bird species should remain immune from pursuit. In its time, this suggestion seemed ridiculous to some of the hunting community. It is now unquestioned.

Finally, American male hunters have been resistant to incorporating women into their ranks, mostly because women have stricter rules about which deaths are necessary for the procurement of food and which are no more than gratuitous, based on fun or the gratification of ego. Men fear women hunters would close down the sorts of hunting that can't be morally justified.

Given this list of grievances, is it possible to reform hunting? One must also ask the larger question: Is hunting *worth* reforming? The first question is one of logistics, the second one of sentiment. Logistically, hunting can be reformed, given what reforms most things: energy, time, and money. However, the real answer to the question of whether hunting is worth reforming depends on how you feel about animals. If you believe that humans can exist without harming animals—that we can evolve to the point that death is removed from the making of our food—then hunting is indeed a relic. If you believe that human and animal life is inextricably linked and that the biology of the planet demands and will continue to demand that some life-forms feed others, then hunting is not only part of that process but also has the potential to serve as a guide to how that process might be most conscientiously and reverentially undertaken.

I believe that hunting can be reformed and is worth reforming, and I offer these suggestions on how to do it. First and foremost, the hunting community and wildlife agencies need to find the money and staff to provide more rigorous hunter-education programs. Biology, forest management, expert marksmanship, and ethics would be covered in far greater depth, and a stiff field and written test passed before a hunting license was issued. Part of this course would examine the pros and cons of ecosystem management and wilderness designation, so that hunters might become a constituency for keeping habitat undeveloped. This will be an extremely difficult task given that a more stringent program will eliminate some hunters, which of course will decrease funding for agencies and profits for the sporting industry. If more stringent hunter education is to succeed, agencies will have to find additional funding besides the current bargain-basement prices of licenses, and the objections of the hunting and outdoor-equipment industries, not eager to lose customers, will have to be met.

Nonetheless, there are ways to overcome the loss of revenue associated with a reduction in the hunting population. A hunting license remains one of the most inexpensive ways to participate in the outdoors in North America today. If, for argument's sake, the number of America's hunters was reduced by half, couldn't license prices be doubled to make up the difference? A deer license that was seventeen dollars would then cost thirty-four dollars and still be a bargain.

Could gun, clothing, and outdoor-equipment manufacturers raise their prices twofold and maintain sales? Unlikely. But outdoor equipment could be taxed, as guns and fishing tackle now are, to produce revenues for wildlife that isn't hunted. As well, a small income tax could be levied for wildlife care and research.

Second, de-emphasize the record book and the pursuit of trophies for the trophy's sake. This is not to say that animals will no longer be admired and taxidermists put out of business. Rather, we would stop valuing animals by so many inches of horn or antler. I would also suggest that if records must be kept as a way of honoring animals that only animals should be listed, not hunters. In addition, hunters might initiate a completely new form of record keeping, one that honored the greatest amount of wildlife habitat conserved.

Third, hunters need to speak out against competitions that involve shooting animals—deer, pigeons, coyotes, prairie dogs, you name it. Such gaming shows a gross disrespect for animals and has nothing to do with hunting.

Fourth, managers and communicators need to reshape the terminology they use. "Sport" and "recreation," the terms that distinguished conservationist hunters like Roosevelt from the market hunters who participated in the decimation of buffalo and waterfowl have become pejorative terms when used with reference to killing animals. They are unacceptable to many in the environmental movement, who are not opposed to hunting if it is done with care, and many nonhunters, including vegetarians, who have been ambivalent about hunting but who can understand the activity as a "least-harm option" when compared to agribusiness and the domestic meat industry. Perhaps hunters can call themselves simply "hunters."

Likewise, the words "consumptive," which has been used to describe hunters, and "nonconsumptive," which has been attributed to birdwatchers and backpackers, need to be discarded. "Consumptive" and "nonconsumptive," like "sport" and "recreation," aren't the most precise terms with which to conceptualize these issues. Should the hunter who hunts a deer ten miles from his home be called a consumptive resource user, and his neighbor who flies ten thousand miles to Antarctica to watch penguins be termed a nonconsumptive user of the planet's resources? The entire hunting debate needs to be reframed in terms of an individual's impacts on regional, national, and global wildlife.

Fifth, the hunting community must open the doors of hunting to women in its practice, its ideas, and its administration. "Man the hunter" has been a great sound bite for anthropologists who believe that hunting has been one of the primary shapers of human character, but women—helping to stampede bison and mammoths over cliffs, skinning animals, making clothing, and gathering vegetables and herbs—worked just as hard, if not harder, to keep the species alive. Indeed, if women anthropologists had been doing most of the research, hunting peoples over most of the temperate globe might have been more accurately labeled "gatherer-hunters" rather than "hunter-gatherers." Either way you read it, both genders contribute to the evolution of our species, and it would be healthy if today they participated more equally in all the tasks of living, from raising children to growing and killing food. Until women restore their sympathies to hunting's fundamental life-giving, life-respecting aspects and have a hand in reducing its elements of machismo and competition, hunters will be fighting an uphill and losing battle. It is women who will vote hunting out of existence.

Sixth, hunters need to participate in more realistic population planning and immigration policy. At current birthrates, along with legal and illegal immigration, the United States will have 380 million people by 2025. There will be far less room left for wildlife. We need to examine our policies on tax credits for bearing children, on teenage sex education, and on the availability of birth control. Ignoring the issue of population growth, as most everyone in North America does, will lead to the inexorable loss of wildlife habitat, wildlife, and public hunting as we know it.

Seventh, hunters need to publicize a more accurate cost accounting of American diets. Millions of North America's hunters hunt locally and put a substantial amount of food, in the form of venison and birds, on their families' tables. In terms of their consumptive effect on the total environment, some of these hunters— who don't use large amounts of fossil fuel to go hunting—can incur less ecological impact than supermarket vegetarians whose entire diet consists of products from America's intensively managed and fossil fuel–dependent industrial farms, where pesticides, combining, and habitat loss cause wildlife to suffer.

To illustrate this idea, one can compare the kilocalorie cost of different diets. An elk shot near a hunter's home in the Rocky Mountains incurs a cost to planet Earth of about eighty thousand kilocalories. This includes the energy to produce the hunter's car, clothing, firearm, and to freeze the elk meat over a year. If the hunter chooses to replace the amount of calories he gets from 150 pounds of elk meat with rice and beans grown in California, the cost to planet Earth is nearly five hundred thousand kilocalories, which includes the energy costs of irrigation, farm equipment, and transportation of the food inland from the coast. It does not include the cost to wildlife—songbirds, reptiles, and small mammals—who are killed as a result of agribusiness. Their deaths make the consumer of agribusiness foods a participant in the culling of wildlife to feed humans.

Even when we understand these trade-offs, it's not always easy to make clear or compassionate choices about our diets. The elk shot in the forest, the tuna netted at sea, the rabbits lost as combines thresh the fields to provide us with our natural breakfast cereals, as well as the Douglas fir hidden in the walls of our homes and the wildlife displaced to light and heat our buildings with fossil fuels or hydropower are all foreclosures. Every day, consciously or not, we close down one life over another, a constant, often unwitting choice of who will suffer so that we may continue living. Given this condition (what one philosopher has called "the condition of being an imperfect being in an imperfectible world") and the difficulty of our escaping from it completely, we may attempt to do the least harm possible to other life. Virtually always, this means finding our food more locally. In some home places, such a discipline would still include hunting, in other home places organic farming, in some places both.

In spite of our differing sentiments about animals, hunters and nonhunters remain in this dynamic system together. All the accusations that may be fairly leveled against the American hunter—greedy, thoughtless, lazy, consumptive, sexist—can also be brought against our culture at large. How can we expect more of the average American hunter, or for that matter inner-city gangs or junk-bond dealers, when they are products of a society that, in its films, politics, work ethic, and recreation, frequently displays these very negative characteristics and in the main has lost a sense of attention, discipline, care, practice, respect, and quality?

This impoverished state exists in part because we have lost our teachers and our holy people. Hunters ought to be in the ranks of both, but unless they find impeccable ways to restore what was a sacred activity, hunting will be, in its depauperated condition, rightfully disparaged and lost. Going out to have fun, I'm afraid, will no longer cut it. In fact, it never did. The humble, grateful, accomplished emotions that surround well-performed hunting cannot be equated with "fun," that which provides amusement or arouses laughter. By "fun" I mean the cruel delight that comes at another's demise, not the celebratory joy inherent in well-performed hunting that produces a gift of food.

If hunters are going to preserve hunting, they must re-create it as the disciplined, mindful, sacred activity it once was for our species. They will also need to help redeem the culture in which they have grown and which finds fun at the expense of others. This is a job for hunters not only as hunters but also as citizens—an ongoing task to define what is appropriate behavior both between people and between what Black Elk, the Oglala Sioux holy man, called the two-leggeds and the four-leggeds. I would say that this definition will have much to do with the notions of kindness, compassion, and sympathy for those other species with whom we share this web of life and upon whom we depend for our sustenance, the very notions—along with restraint—that informed the lives of some hunting peoples in times past.

Such a reformation—or rather a return to older principles of mutual regard between species—will be a profound undertaking, for it is based on the pre-Christian belief that other life-forms, indeed the very plants and earth and air themselves, are invested with soul and spirit. If we must take those spirits, it can only be done for good reason and then only if accompanied by constant reverence and humility for the sacrifices that have been made. Whether we're hunters or nonhunters, meat eaters or vegetarians, this state of heart and mind compels us to say an eternal grace.

Facing up to this basic and poignant condition of biological life on this planet—people, animals, and plants as fated cohorts, as both dependents and donors of life—wasn't easy ten thousand years ago and won't be today. Of course, we can back away from the task, but I think the result would be either a world in which people continue to dominate nature or a world in which simplistic notions of how to reduce pain sever the bonds between people and nature. In either case, we will remain distant from the complex burdens and daily sympathy that some ancient hunters considered the basis for a loving community of people and animals.

Can this reformation really be accomplished without the participatory context of gathering and hunting that informed our species for thousands of years? Can we know the old knowledge of those times even though many of us spend our lives far from the animals and plants who sustain us? I doubt it, unless we attempt to restore participation. Many of us may never have the privilege to harvest wheat we have grown, skin a deer we have killed, or fillet a fish we have caught. Virtually all of us, though, have a window and a piece of sky. We can choose to grow salad greens or a few herbs. Though a small gesture of participation in the world that feeds us, putting one's hands in a small pot of dirt, emblem of the original ground from which we have sprung, is a powerful thing to do and a beginning. If we are hunters or anglers, I will suggest that it is our first duty to introduce non-hunters and non-anglers to the participatory context. In short, take a child, a friend, a spouse hunting or fishing and don't be ashamed to show that reverence for life goes hand in hand with the taking of it.

It is time to stop the rhetorical protection of hunting. It is time to nurture and restore the spirit that informed it. Such a commitment, if followed diligently, would certainly close down hunting as a sport. It would maintain it, though, as one of our important and fundamental weddings with nature.

KNOWING NOVEMBER

1

In silky spouts, my breath joined the stars. The dark ridges of
pine and spruce lay before me, and the valley, smoothed by
September, October, and now November snow, walked easily,
sage buried, tangles erased, the tire-tamped road meandering far
below, along the frozen river pointing toward the Tetons, jagged
and remote. To the east, a surf line of peaks, the Wind Rivers,
broke. In between, the forests and crumbling cliffs of the Gros
Ventres rose and fell, rose and fell, black and white, home
ground.

The trail turned up along the snout of a ridge. A runnel of
elk prints led toward the stars—cow prints the size of my palm,
like upside-down hearts split open through the middle, with the
diminutive tracks of calves by their sides. Here and there, a larger
bull print wandered, cutting across the trough. Though the rut
was long over, this bull seemed to be looking for a cow in estrus.
His tracks made the rounds, indicating his exploration of the

rumps climbing before him. A set of boot prints also walked among the trail, coming down the ridge the opposite way. Not a surprise—they were mine, from the previous afternoon when I had gained the ridge a thousand feet higher and from the next valley over.

Sitting under a solitary white bark pine, I had listened. The highway of elk tracks had narrowed a few hundred yards farther up the ridge and entered the black, north-facing timber.

Merle, the golden Lab, sat by my side and stared into the trees. His ears made the tiniest twitch forward, his shoulders quivered minutely. Slowly, he turned his head and looked at me knowingly.

"Elk?" I whispered.

He made the slightest affirmative whine, looked back.

We sat. The sun set. The northern Winds went the color of wild roses. The Tetons became irises turned to stone. In the pink and lavender light, like the sound of the first star, a bugle floated down the ridge.

Merle turned his head over his shoulder.

His eyes said, "See."

I sighed. Not because he can hear more than I. It hadn't snowed in a week and what lay underfoot was like insulation board, cracking at the slightest step. Without much hope, we started up the elk tracks, walking in them where they had frozen, to minimize the noise.

Luckily, the evening breeze crossed the trail at a ninety-degree angle. We entered the trees, skirted the edge of a canyon, regained the ridge crest, and there—so suddenly that it was like walking into a wall—their smell began: barnyard gone wild, musk mixed with fir and wind. Through the trees, I could see the sky, and against the sky I could see the rufous shapes of elk, now moving, for they had heard us.

They were maybe thirty yards off, which made me feel good, getting that close in that kind of snow. And I could have shot, but they were moving nervously behind the screening trees toward the ridge top's final meadow. So I ran, angling down and away so I'd come up alongside them in the meadow itself, if they decided to slow down.

When I ran into the open, the elk were trotting across the park's far end: two dozen cows, heads high, nostrils flared; a dozen calves; and one six-point bull in the rear. I just watched, for it was one of those shots that was wrong from the start: the elk spooked and full of adrenalin; the first of them already in the timber with miles of it before them; the rest of them so closely packed that it would be difficult to hold surely on one animal; and dark less than an hour away.

But my mind was already beyond the lost opportunity to shoot, following the elk into the steep and tangled north-facing trees where, if I stayed put and did nothing more, they would stop, wait, and probably return to this meadow or the one below it to graze during the night.

Sitting in the snow, Merle and I listened to them move through the forest, breaking branches as they circled around the head of the canyon. When they came even with us on the opposite rim and caught our wind, the bull bugled—once, twice, a long pause, then a third time. Then the sky became a mute, still blue, accompanied by the evening drop in temperature. We waited in the cold, but the elk were still as well. A single star came out, minute and straight overhead. We began to walk down the ridge, and I thought, looking at the stands of pine, the hidden swales, about our route back up it in the morning.

Now, after a few hours' sleep, we were back. The ridge flattened and widened before us. Sage meadows, separated by stands of lodgepole pine, rose toward Orion. As always, when limited by increasing or decreasing light, the stalker's decision is based on knowing when to make time and when to be disciplined.

Someplace, ahead and above me, the elk were probably grazing. A few of them would be looking down the ridge and would see any erect human climbing up it. The erect human could crawl but probably wouldn't get to the elk before the sun had risen and they had sifted back into the forest.

So I climbed rapidly, noticing the color coming onto the eastern Winds, climbed without worrying about the noise, with my binoculars hanging in my jacket and my rifle slung over my shoulder. Just below the first place I reckoned the elk would be, I chambered a cartridge, took out my glasses, then bent low and continued on with greater stealth. Not a minute later, as I came over a slight rise, I saw three elk skylighted on the crest of the ridge—black shapes against a crystalline violet sky. They were looking at me and saw me bent over for not more than a second or two—maybe I was a coyote, maybe a deer—before I was down on the snow and out of sight, circling left into the pines, Merle at my heels.

Ahead, the ridge became shaped like a wishbone. The three elk I had seen were on its right fork. I was moving up the left. In between was a meadow of willow where I figured the other elk were grazing. Once, I peeked over the crest and saw them: a dozen shapes bedded in the dwarf willow, with a half dozen more shapes grazing, the tireless bull still courting two cows. Studying the way ahead, I saw that if I continued up alongside the ridge I was upon, screened by its crest, I could crawl over the top just about even with the feeding elk, lie prone, and have a shot of a hundred or so yards.

The geometry of the stalk, and the fact that the elk were feeding where I had thought they would be, pleased me enormously. There is nothing quite like seeing yourself as a diviner of events in your home country, events in whose outcome you have a large investment, then having your predictions validated. For a moment, actually longer than a moment as I crawled through the snow, I lost my concentration and indulged myself in an appreciation of my own skill, first in my ability to find wildlife and then in my ability to shoot well. I thought about how I had killed this year's deer with one shot, and last year's elk with one shot, and last year's deer with one shot as well, which was a good string of careful hunting and fine shooting that had ended two years in which no stalk had gone really well and I had taken two, three, and even four shots to make the year's meat.

Since I was a child, I have always enjoyed this sort of calculation, keeping records of both my performance in the field—so many shots taken to so many birds in the hand, so many fish hooked to so many landed—as well as tracking the comings and goings of fish and animals. Long before I took a college biology course and learned about keeping a field journal, I had had one. After a while, looking at my notes, I came to see patterns: that mullet ran up the creeks within a few days of when they did it the year before and the year before that, and that striped bass of course followed them, congregating at the very low tides of a new or a full moon, which made it easier for them to herd and catch the mullet. Making it my business to wade in those tide rips on just such nights, I gained the reputation of being prescient when it was no more than being observant. And given my empirical frame of mind, I carefully weighed and measured the fish, even those I released, believing that numbers could give me an idea of how successful I was.

Later, when I started to hunt large mammals, I followed the

same practice, pacing off the shots I made, counting how many times I fired and hit and how many times I fired and missed, believing once again that I would learn something from the exercise—see patterns, become a better shot—and also because, among the older men who were my role models, I preferred those who were honest.

So much of fishing and hunting is done alone, in private, that it is easy for even the most careful person to create a mythology for himself, to make himself "a legend in his own mind," as a friend once put it, to remember the well done and forget the poorly rendered. I say "himself" because among outdoor people I have known, including the climbers, skiers, and boaters, this is much more a male habit than a female one.

You can't do this in baseball. Your batting average, your earned run average, are there for everyone to see. You can't do this in business either, at least not for very long, because your performance is evaluated. You can't even do this in a relationship with a partner who is self-confident—eventually such a person calls you on your nonsense.

But out there alone in the field, it's amazing how easy it is to soften the past, framing its uncomfortable details out of sight, like those calendar shots of majestic mountains that delete the condos at their base. And unlike condos, your own poor performance, framed out of sight long enough, actually disappears.

Unless, that is, you write it down and look at it again. Last year, when I reviewed my data from eleven seasons, I was surprised. I had considered myself a disciplined and attentive hunter, a Zen sort of guy when it came to being mindful about shooting at animals. But the statistics didn't completely bear out my opinion. Over those past eleven seasons I had fired at twenty-six different white-taileds, mule deer, pronghorn, caribou, and elk—mostly elk. I had killed twenty-one of these animals, or 81 percent. I had missed five cleanly. These twenty-one animals took thirty-five shots to kill, an average of 1.66 shots per animal, which sounds pretty good given the many variables of shooting in the mountains as compared to shooting at the target range with its bench rests and known distances: the quirky wind; the sometimes moving animals; the sometimes winded, tired, and excited hunter; his or her sometimes imprecise estimate of the range; and the less-than-ideal shooting positions the terrain demands—flopped in the snow, wrapped around a tree, not infrequently merely on the wobbly hind legs evolution has given us. Of course, you can't ever forget how the rifle is influenced by the tidal buffet of your heart's pulse, periodically destroying what momentary steadiness you achieve. It is a wonder that anyone hits anything, and, in fact, many never do. The national success rate for elk hunters is somewhat less than 20 percent.

Indeed, including the animals I had missed, it was more accurate to say that I had taken forty-six shots to kill twenty-one animals, which meant that I had missed sixteen times overall, never hitting what I had aimed at 35 percent of the time. Looking at that number from its obverse, I had hit what I aimed at only 65 percent of the time. I guess this is better than batting .300, which people get paid a lot of money to do, but seeing that number appear on my calculator's display dispelled any notion that I was Mr. Cool Marksman. In fact, most of my misses occurred after I had shot once and hit. Firing again, I would miss once or twice on the running animal, and, finally settling down, kill it. To put all these numbers in perspective, I also had to consider the following: thirteen out of the twenty-one animals I had killed took one shot; three out of the twenty-one took two shots; two of the twenty-one took three cartridges; and three of the twenty-one required four bullets to bring down—not that I actually hit these three animals four times each; the two middle shots were always misses. Fortunately, during all this time—in fact, not once during my entire life—had I ever wounded and lost an animal. This pleased me about as much as my stalking skill and rattled me more than a bit. As any statistician will tell you, the probability of maintaining a streak decreases the longer it goes on.

When I came over the rise, pushing my pack before me, the dawn was still far-off. The meadow, a quarter mile square of willow, was a dull gray, dotted by the darker shapes of the elk. I pushed my pack alongside a rock that was higher than my head, rested the rifle over the pack, and looked at the elk through my binoculars. Merle lay behind me. The bull swung his head at the two cows; I could see some of the bedded animals chewing their cuds; on the ridge, the three sentinel elk stood watch. I had checked the thermal drift with my lighter, and, as usual in the early morning, the night's cold air floated down the mountain—from the elk to me. But in one of those impossible-to-predict developments that happen all the time in the high country, some wayward current swirled my scent back up the ridge and down into the meadow. I could tell that this had happened by how the elk looked uphill from where we lay, then slowly looked down the ridge, still seeing nothing, but now uneasy. Or perhaps it was just our presence, no more than our physically lying on the ridge where there had been no creatures before, that changed everything.

One by one they stood, beginning to drift, like seedpods borne by a slow and steady wind, toward the opposite side of the meadow and up toward the three sentinels. One cow, the closest to me, quartered away, her right flank exposed. She was no more than a 150 yards off, and I snugged the rifle into my shoulder, found her in the scope, and tracked her. She was moving at a slow

walk, but if possible I prefer a standing animal. As if the thought
had gone from my head to hers, she stopped. I said my apologies,
my thanks, began the slow squeeze of the trigger. And she
moved—slowly, but nonetheless moved. I waited and then I
wished that I had shot. For, climbing the opposite ridge, she exposed only her back, a shot that would ruin too much meat. She
crossed behind some trees, and when she reemerged she was as
far off as the three guards—275 yards. The other elk had filtered
toward the head of the meadow, more than four hundred yards
from me.

I lay there and thought, thought about it all—the season coming to a close and my having gotten up so many mornings in the
dark; my having climbed to the ridge tops so many times; having
not shot on three or four reasonable occasions because I wanted
to keep being out there, hunting; having looked at the freezer,
which now had about five pounds of burger left; and having seen
on the calendar the end of the season approaching too quickly,
like a highway exit that I hadn't anticipated. I have never believed
that the world would be perfect, only happy and sometimes bit-
tersweet. And I've always been willing to try what I imagined I
could do well.

Aiming at the last sentry elk in line, who was broadside and
absolutely still, I said my farewells. Still, she didn't move. I let out
half a breath and tried to elongate the tidal pool of quiet between each stroke of my heart. The rifle lay steady, and then it
boomed—frightening and flashing orange in the dim light. I
thought I heard the bullet hit, maybe. But there the three elk
stood. The elk in the meadow fled into the timber. The three
lookouts wheeled and dropped over the far side of the ridge.
This was astonishing. At this range, from such a position with
this particular scope-sighted rifle, I had never missed.

Still incredulous, I stood up, looked at the rifle, actually tried to wiggle the scope. Solid. Putting on my pack and followed by Merle, I walked down through the sage, across the willow, up the other slope, and on to the top of the ridge.

Snow, windswept tundra, lichen-colored rocks. Not a spot of blood. I walked up and down the ridge several times, its crest now illuminated by the brightening eastern sky. I looked carefully down its other side, following the running tracks of the elk with my eyes and my binoculars. Nothing. I looked to where I had shot. Staring back across the meadow, less than three football fields wide, the distance seemed even closer.

At that range, with this rifle, a dead-on hold in the top part of an elk's chest kills an elk. (And I remembered the crosshairs precisely there.) Having shot this rifle several thousand times at the range, I knew this like I knew my own name. But there was no dead elk on the ridge where there should have been a dead elk. And there was no blood, even though I thought that I had heard the bullet hit.

Feeling a sickening weight in my stomach, I started down the opposite side of the ridge, through the deep snow, seeing no more than the tracks of three healthily running elk, which soon joined a great confusion of tracks. Unknown to me, there had been other elk, grazing on the far side of the ridge.

As Merle and I descended to the first trees, trying to follow the tracks of the three running elk, an elk bedded within the pines jumped up and bounded away—no more than sixty yards off. I threw up the rifle, but so sure had I been that I couldn't have missed the elk whom I had fired upon—indeed, that I would find her fallen dead on the other side of the ridge—that I hadn't worked a fresh round into the chamber.

Feeling utterly stupid and undone, I chambered a cartridge.

Merle looked at me as if I were out of my mind. We hurried to her bed and found no blood in the oval depression, nor any blood in her departing tracks. Was this an elk I had wounded, or another elk, bedded on this side of the ridge? Surrounding her bed and crisscrossed through the trees were so many tracks that it was impossible to tell. But I felt it unlikely that an elk would have remained bedded here amid the confusion and noise of running elk above and around her had she not been wounded.

I began to follow her tracks through the forest, along a steep sidehill, across a meadow, easily distinguishing her galloping prints until they found the tracks of the rest of the herd, which descended from the willow above and started off on a long-used elk run. Now it became nearly impossible to separate this elk's tracks from all the others, but I continued to follow, hoping that I would find a dead elk and knowing that I wouldn't.

The elk trail led me upward through steep spruce and fir. There I found the tiniest smudge of blood on a tree that had fallen across the trail and precisely where many elk knees had rubbed the bark smooth as they leapt over the obstacle. Was it from the elk I was following or another one? The trail took me across a knoll where old elk beds had been melted into the snow, up another steep forested slope, and into the very meadow where Merle and I had stalked the herd less than twenty-four hours before. The trail I followed joined the trail of the previous night and went into the north woods—an old escape route and one filled with tangled deadfall and blown-down trees.

Feeling confused and unsure, I sat on a stump and drank a cup of tea. I looked at the sky and the mountains. I visualized the picture of my sight as the rifle boomed, and what I recollected as the sound of the bullet hitting. I could not believe that I had grazed the elk in the knee or even missed completely. Instead, I must have missed some clue. I walked back down the ridge and searched the spot where the elk had been. They had stood on snow and any blood should have shown like a stain on a white linen suit. But there was truly nothing. I dropped off the ridge, making widening circles through the forest, trying to find where the tracks of the three elk went after they had entered the trees. I lost them in the many other prints. Then I followed the track of the bedded elk, hoping to see where she might have turned downhill, finding an easier way, as she might have been expected to do had she been badly wounded. No luck and no blood other than the one smudge.

By the afternoon, feeling frustrated and low, I went home, slept fitfully, constantly turning over the shot in my mind, came back early the next morning, and reenacted the entire stalk, then followed the spoor until it was impossible to say what spoor I was following. All the time I wondered, "If I had wounded the elk whom I had shot at, was the wound superficial, mortal, or something in between?" But I could find no evidence of any of these contingencies. Except for the memory of the bedded elk jumping up and running away, the position of my crosshairs, and my recollection of the sound of the bullet hitting, there was nothing.

Nothing.

There is nothing worse than nothing—that state of guilt and quasi-hope, mental flagellation and constant replaying of every detail, wishing to find something that I had overlooked and always finding an unknown and an accusation: I had become too prideful, way too prideful, smug, and cocky, and had shot too far.

II

When you are single and have gone through too many relation-ships that have started in hope and ended with hard feelings, there is great peace in the mountains. Empty of your friends' and family's expectations, they let you converse clearly with yourself, especially in November when the world is turning somnolent, when the solstice is still weeks away, when the headiness and hope of spring are too far behind and too far ahead to hold. Then, if you are honest, you can see clearly the choices you have made. They become dichromatic, like the black-and-white land-scape of fir and snow: this choice or that; to shoot or not; to be-come involved with this person or that; the ownership of choice and deed held within your own will. In November, in the moun-tains, the world is too empty to find anyone else to blame.

I walked through the snow, thinking about my two hunting partners, both married and in bed while I was out here in the dark. It is easy in the very early morning, in the low biorhythm of the day, to find yourself filled with character flaws that make you an outcast, that turn what you considered your discipline into pigheadedness, your well-earned pride into hubris, your love of quiet and empty spaces into a curmudgeon's isolation; and all because of a promise broken. To shoot well, to never wound, and to have failed. Or at least this was the most recent failure to gnaw and worry at.

The snow fell, and I walked in the dim light, making a long, familiar circle through the stands of pine and aspen. For some mixture of reasons—the wind, the half-blizzardy conditions, how I felt in my bones about myself that day—I knew I wouldn't see elk. But it didn't matter. It was enough to be out in the storm, the weather like a psalm.

When the morning clouds became bright enough, I went home, fed the horses, worked at my desk as the snow continued to fall, the afternoon came, the night cleared, and the morning broke, cloudless. I slept in, tired and wanting to be fresh.

In the afternoon, I headed back upriver and climbed to my spotting knoll at the fork of two valleys, both of which had given me many elk and deer. Putting on several layers of clothing, I sat and watched. The world was as silent as a world can be—rivers frozen, snow muffling the ground, trees drawn into themselves with the subzero cold. A raven quorked like a koan in the sky.

In a circle that measured three quarters of the horizon, I glassed the ridges and parks. Merle sat by my side, but after an hour of glassing, he sighed. Turning, he made a bed in the snow and lay against me. A mover not a sitter, he groaned softly with impatience.

For the twentieth, thirtieth, or perhaps fortieth time, I swept the binoculars across the ridges, and where no elk had been an elk now stood, watching the world. I could see her with my unaided eye, two drainages away, the drainages separated by a spine of forest. To reach her, I had to go down to the creek below me, across the spine, down into another small valley, and up a long bare ridge, atop which stood the elk. Three quarters of a mile, by line of sight. There would be just enough time.

Taking off my heavy clothing, I stuffed it into my pack. Merle was on his feet, wagging his tail. We foot-skied down the slope, thigh deep in powder, broke trail through the sage, found a way among the tall trees. In the next park, I checked the wind—downhill—and began the long climb up the side of the ridge.

The top of the ridge ran perpendicularly before me, eventually meeting the forested spine that Merle and I had crossed minutes before. Between the two was a narrow steep canyon, treed on one side, bare on the other (the bare side was the one I was now climbing), and where the trees and the bare steep slope met, there was another knoll, this valley's lookout. My head came around to it, as did Merle's, not because I had planned on examining it, but because of the smell that wafted down from it.

Elk.

Three bedded at its top, about five hundred yards off and above us, chewing their cuds and staring over the frozen valley. And so still was the air and so sure the drift, that we had smelled them from that far off. We shrank into the trees along whose edge we had been climbing and watched the animals. They hadn't seen us.

I wondered if one of them was the elk whom I had seen from two valleys away and who had wandered back along the ridge to join her companions. In the time that had elapsed, this would have been more than possible. The stalk now presented itself like a forty-five-degree right triangle. We had to climb up one leg of the triangle, drop over the crest of the intervening ridge, proceed about halfway up the other leg, crawl to the top of the ridge again, and shoot at the elk who lay across the small canyon and midway on the hypotenuse.

But the first leg was exposed. Merle and I cut through the trees and, screened by them, made a long wayward circle away from the elk. The slope steepened and became wind scoured. I kicked steps in the snow. To the west, the sun had gone behind the Tetons, the snow before us turning the color of pink carnations, the sky overhead grading from lavender to dusky purple. Methodically, I kicked steps while Merle walked behind me, a long climbing traverse away from the elk, hurrying but not hurrying, and without any thoughts now, just lost in the swing of each foot into the hard surface of the dying-pink snow.

Approaching the top of the ridge, the cover of the trees long gone, I bent low, my crouch keeping the summit of the ridge just above the elk's line of sight. After foot-skiing down the far side, I stood, took the rifle from my shoulder, and walked easily through the deep snow of the lee side, thinking about the three elk whom I was stalking but also about the single elk whom I had first seen on this ridge and who might still be about.

The shallow plateau to our left held small stands of pine, and there was a large stand of pines ahead, not quite halfway to the spot on the ridge where I planned to crawl over its top. Walking toward this copse of trees, we dropped into a swale and when we came up its other side, an elk stood before us, not forty yards off. Behind it, bedded in the pines, were fifteen more elk, all cows and calves. I was almost certain that the standing elk was the one whom I had seen from across the valley, almost an hour before.

She looked at us. I raised the rifle, hesitating, sending my thoughts to her. She stood without moving, standing broadside, and I fired.

After the shot, she remained motionless, then turned and ran. The rest of the herd stood and followed. Working the bolt, I followed her in the sight, fired again, and she tumbled. Her legs jerked as if she were still running, and then she lay still.

Her herd ran by her, up the valley—one cow looking back, waiting and reluctant to leave, then trotting off as she saw Merle bounding toward her. He didn't chase. He sniffed the fallen elk all over, then, tail going like a whip, watched me approach. I walked around the elk, making sure that she wouldn't jump up, then I sat by her shoulder. Merle sat on her opposite side, both of us watching her energy—erectile in each hair, in each eyelash, on the bright curve of her eye—begin to evaporate into the cold air and seep into the snow. One of the old songs—when words were still howls, growls, yips—came from my mouth, sending her spirit on its way, taking it in.

"Fly on, fly on, you who feed us. You who scent our breath, who shape our limbs, who let us see. What can we say of this trade that is no trade? What thanks can be made when we still have the world that you've been taken from? What song might we sing till our bones feed your children? Fly on, fly on, you who make us. Fly on."

I rolled her over and saw one neat hole through her chest. The first shot had missed, which seemed improbable, but which could only be true. I pondered this, wondering why I was so poorly focused, and knowing the answer.

It was long after dark when I got home and bright sunshine when I awoke. As she had asked me to do a few weeks ago, I called her. She had wanted to help carry out my elk, which was her way of saying that she was no longer angry. I wasn't so sure how I felt. Not that we had been intimately involved. We had shared some horses, disagreed about their care, and each thought the other stubborn and selfish. She had taken her horse away, and we hadn't spoken for months.

Now, on the way up, each of us leading a packsaddled mount, she talked about the man who had broken her heart and the woman whom he had married and how they were unhappy, which she had known was going to happen from the start. She sounded fiercely vindicated.

Once I had thought that this woman with her cowboy hat and silky brown hair, with her horses and dogs, would get over this man, and we would be partners, because we liked so many of the same things—horses, mountains, and kids—but here she was, still working herself into a lather over him, two years gone. And I began to regret having agreed to her coming along.

Then we came over the top of the ridge and walked down to the dead elk, gutted but not skinned. As I took out my knife and meat saw, she stood before the fallen elk, a cloud of silence on her face, muteness in her entire frame. Her posture seemed to say, This is another . . . wounded female. All of a sudden, that is exactly how I felt about how she felt about herself and the elk at our feet—that they were both casualties of the world's remorselessness.

She knelt by the side of the elk and touched her hide. Running her hand over the elk's cape where the black mane met the shorter and thicker brown hair of the shoulders, she seemed to go into a trance, staring so deeply into the elk's body that it was hard to distinguish where elk left off and woman began. She knelt for several minutes more before pressing the elk's shoulder with great calmness, letting something go out of her fingers—a splinter of pain, a chasm of anger, something shared and measureless and somehow healing.

Looking up, she said, "Can I help?"

I gave her a leg to hold and began to skin. Later, she took the hide in her hands, clasping its fatty underside unabashedly. Then we sawed the elk into quarters, she holding the legs while I sawed and boned out the meat. She asked the occasional question about which cuts became steaks and which burger and how they were to be frozen. And once she said, her voice sounding like the appearance of the first star, like her voice had come out of nowhere but had been there all day, "She is so beautiful."

I looked at her, feeling all my expectations finally gone—the woman whom I had wanted and created in my mind gone and just a person in her moment before me, a person who loved mountains and kids and horses and with whom I had shared some fine times, this one more, and that was enough.

"It's good to see you," I said.

When we had folded the skin into a packable bundle and placed the meat in the panniers, I went to a nearby pine and hung a string of Tibetan prayer flags in its branches. Just across the valley was the place on the ridge where, last week, I had wounded or missed the elk. The flags, which are white, green, yellow, blue, and red—ether, air, earth, water, and fire—were for that elk and for this one: carried from Tibet, blessed by a lama on the other side of the planet, inscribed with words that would be faded by sunlight and borne away by wind, "Behold the jewel in the lotus flower"; not much for the lives I had taken to feed my life, but in such times there isn't anything else you can say except your brand of prayer.

We loaded the panniers on the horses, and I left the head and hooves on a small rise, looking north, where I said a few more words with them. Then we led the horses up the ridge.

"Mind if I have a moment?"

She took the horses off, and I crouched in the snow, Merle coming behind me to sit. I stared down the valley, which had given me several years' worth of hunting. Some of those stalks and shooting had been as unmarred, as pure as new fallen snow. Others had been like snow at the end of the year, pitted, rotten, caving underfoot, demanding care to find the way over the still-solid bridges. Why did one or the other happen? I looked at the red splotch of snow a few hundred yards below me. Maybe it was how well you could totally concentrate—not just saying you were concentrating with your mind and your senses, but concentrating with all your heart, which meant it too had to be at peace, not tugging and longing. But I also knew that some of the most graceful moments of my life—not only hunting but skiing and writing—had taken place when my heart was not at peace with itself. As in the moment when you shoot, suspending your breath and feeling the still point between your pulse, so too must a heart learn to calm itself even while troubled.

I picked up some snow, rubbed it on my face, rubbed it on Merle's, and standing and turning, cast it to the four winds.

She was staring at the Tetons, too white and ethereal to be of this earth, too shattered and solid to be of anyplace else.

"Thanks for inviting me," she said. Staring at the mountains, she didn't turn to look at me. "It makes you quiet."

She handed me a lead rope and we started down.

III

Scott, who is about as quiet and stolid as a forest, went across and up the Buffalo River, to a spot that I had showed him on the map. It was his first year hunting, and the way he does economics he did his hunting. Without much fanfare he bought a rifle, took it to the range, and practiced. He borrowed several books on shooting and elk hunting from me and read them. He asked sensible questions and pondered my answers, pushing back his hat from his copper-colored hair, his blue eyes entertaining other variables.

He went across and up the Buffalo in the very early morning, leaving his wife, April, sleeping in their bed, and his new daughter, Tessa, sleeping in her crib. He hiked in the dark, in the deep, still cold of late November, and sat on a bench high above the river. At dawn, a cow elk walked within twenty-five feet of him, and he shot her once through the chest, gutted her, and dragged her down to the road by himself. He is a neat and pragmatic sort of guy, strong as well, which is also necessary to drag out a whole elk by yourself.

My other hunting partner, Benj, didn't like getting up early or walking far. Rotund, shaped like a Persian rug dealer, with a graying mustache and sly Eurasian eyes, Benj diddled and haggled over rifles, as if maybe he was buying dancing girls, decided to shoot one cartridge for deer and pronghorns and another for elk, killed both a deer and a pronghorn in September, and by October had given his neighbors so many barbecues that he didn't have a pound of meat left. He has a big heart if not very much pragmatism.

Then he discovered that elk hunting was harder than hunting for deer or pronghorns. The snow was deep, the mornings cold, and the elk lived in more difficult country, staying high in the mountains and forcing you to walk a long way, which meant you had to be in shape. Benj, like Scott, went up along the Buffalo, but long after the sun had risen. He walked uphill in broad daylight, cut the trail of a wounded elk, and, in one of those gestures that makes us all love him though doubt his good sense, followed it, making someone else's work his own. He followed it all day, higher and higher, farther and farther back, wearing himself out so he could do the "humane thing," as he later said, and put the elk out of its misery. He wore out the yearling cow elk before she wore out him. When he reached her, she could barely jump from her bed and turned to look at her pursuer with eyes that said, "I wish you would have let me lie, go to sleep, and feed the coyotes." Feeling wretched but committed to what he thought was the right course of action, Benj shot her and felt even worse.

He came by my place that night, exhausted, unshaven, wild-eyed, like an innkeeper dragged out by the cavalry, and told me the whole story, wanting to know if he had done the right thing with this, his first elk.

I gave him a hug and said that a person did what he thought was right at the moment.

Wretched, he repeated what he had been saying, "She just wanted to go to sleep."

"But you didn't know that from far off."

"Would you have tracked her?"

It is not exactly comfortable to have become a hunting mentor to your friends. They start to believe you have the answers.

"I wouldn't have done it," I said.

"See," he said.

"I wouldn't have done it because I'm selfish, Benj. I want more meat than a yearling elk."

For a moment I thought about our pack trip last summer and my being astonished that Benj would put fly dope on the horses but forget to water them. At first I thought that Benj wasn't really concerned about the horses' welfare and that I was. But at the heart of the matter, he really was concerned, though his priorities weren't always in the right order. On the other hand, though I was concerned about the horses' welfare, it wasn't by any means an unconditional concern. I wanted to ride out of the mountains. For Benj, riding or walking, getting stranded twenty-five miles from the trailhead, his own safety and comfort, didn't matter. It really didn't. He never thought about himself at all.

"I'm always thinking of myself, Benj. You never do."

"I'll never do it again," he said.

There was no sentiment in his voice, no self-pity, just a knowledge about how things are, a knowledge that he had come to by tracking an animal through the snow all day, originally wanting to make some food and mixing up that motive with trying to be Dr. Kevorkian with a rifle.

He stood up, gave me another hug.

"Janny says to take the horses back now."

Janet was Benj's wife, a shaman and a healer, also a hunter.

"She says that if we take the horses to the winter range, then she'll go out and shoot an elk the next morning."

"Don't we have to pack out your elk first?"

He gave me a startled look. "Oh, yeah. I totally forgot. She's still out there."

It was a beautiful evening when we fetched her, the sky a sublime, outer-space blue, the horses' withers and our own mustaches covered with frost. The elk lay nearly two hours' ride up the ridge, through very deep snow, and I said, "Jesus, Benj, did you trail her way up here?"

"Yeah, is it far?"

"Yeah, it really is."

That made him feel good.

He had shot her once through the chest and, when she didn't die, once through the head, which had bugged out her eyes. It was an awful sight, and miserable at seeing her again, he said, "I thought I was doing the humane thing."

"Benj, you'll eat her, she'll be tasty, and you'll stop beating yourself up."

"And I'll never shoot an elk in the head again."

"Or follow someone else's blood trail," I added lightly.

He shrugged, a deep shrug that came out of his bones, his shrug saying that maybe he wouldn't, but maybe, just maybe, given the right circumstances, he would. We follow different hearts.

We skinned and quartered her, fitted her in two panniers, and rode down through the forest, the light dim. As we came into the open, our mounts snorted. The valley was aglitter with trillions of ice crystals suspended in the air as silently as before the first word, before history. The full moon rose in the east, improbably large and orange as a pumpkin; to the west the Tetons—heavy with snow—turned the color of wild roses. Merle bounded ahead as if he would become airborne and soar into the valley below, and the horses followed.

Riding down the slope, surfing through the spume of luminescent twilight, I sensed that mountains and elk, people, horses, and dogs, had become different expressions of the same elements, of the same energy. Though I was bundled in parka and hat, I felt my edges dissolve and melt into the country—someday mountain, once a moon, now a person; in no more than a moment, pushing grass, I'd become those whom I'd hunted.

That was Tuesday. On Wednesday, Benj and I trailered the pack string to the other side of the Wind Rivers and pastured them in the flowing creeks and tall grass of the mountains' snow shadow. On Thursday, Benj and Janet rose early, went upriver, and Janet shot an elk.

She called at eleven.

"Hey, Ted." Her drawl sounded in my ear, and I could imagine her standing at the phone, in her down parka and moon boots, long red hair in a ponytail, cheeks bright with cold.

"Yeah, Princess." I used her nickname, given to her on the Alaska Peninsula when she had remained supine until eleven while the rest of us watched bears.

"Hey, Ted, I got me an elk."

"Just like you said."

"Just like I said. I dreamed it."

"And now you want me to help you carry it out."

"You bet," she laughed. "I was never gonna get an elk when those old horses were around. Too easy."

So I met her at the junction, with a bunch of my frame packs and toboggans. It was Thanksgiving Day, and she had rustled up some neighbors, along with her eleven-year-old, Grant, from her first marriage, to help. We set out in a line, breaking trail through the deep snow and dragging the sleds, and she told me about it.

"I was ahead of Benji, walking down that ridge where you got your elk. And I heard them first, the cows calling. So I waited for him, and we snuck up on 'em, and saw four sets of ears. And the four of them walked away, just a little, and one cow stood broad-side, presenting herself, so to speak, just standing there as if she were waiting for me. I shot her offhand, one shot at eighty yards, and I saw it on her face. She looked like she was thinking, 'Uh-oh, I've been hit.' Then she looked like she thought, 'I don't feel so good. I'm just going to walk over here a ways,' which she did. Then she looked like she was saying, 'I'm just going to lie down here a little bit.' And her knees folded and she lay down. When I got to her, she was breathing her last. I sat by her head, and there was just a little blood in her mouth."

She gave me a sidelong look, mischievous yet absolutely been-there and done-that, this woman with the Playmate figure who had wrangled horses, had a kid, got divorced, worked as a UPS driver, rolled her truck, broke her spine, recovered, and became a practitioner of a Chinese healing art called jin shin jyutsu, before marrying my friend.

"That was it," she said.

"That's a lot."

"Naw." She put on her wrangler look, like she was going to spit some chew. "Just all in a morning's work, haw haw." Suddenly, she let her body go limp, as if she'd fall down on the spot. "Shit, I'm exhausted."

We hiked into the wind, blowing a ground blizzard of powder, out of which Benj emerged—black hat, jacket, and pants—

a big furry figure, carrying the elk's heart and liver. Janet took out a thermos of tea. We ate some sandwiches, and while the group rerigged their packs and sleds, I walked ahead.

When I reached Janet's elk, I found that Benj had quartered her neatly, the meat wrapped in a plastic tarp, the hide laid over everything like a blanket. The head was a ways off, resting on her four hooves, just the way I do it. When I took off the hide and tarp, it was nothing like how I do it, which is to make a rough-and-ready go of it and worry about the details later. It was the neatest quartering job I'd ever seen, the meat looking like it had come out of an anatomy class—perfectly clean, almost bloodless, the fat removed, every ragged end trimmed. It was Benj's way, I thought, to make amends for his elk.

I loaded a hindquarter on my pack and dropped off the ridge to the north. We had come up the southern valley, but the northern one was closer to the road. Just as Merle and I reached the snowmobile track, Benj came up it with his four-by-four. I put the meat in the back, and Merle and I got in the front.

"That was the best skinning and quartering job I've ever seen, Benj."

He looked at me. "Really?"

"Really."

He beamed, totally pleased. Then his face went into the place that is right on the boundary between bitter and sweet, right in the shadow land between what is ideal and what is given, right where your honesty is constantly buffeted by humility on one side and pride on the other. Where it all connects.

CARNIVORE, OMNIVORE, VEGAN: THE HARDEST QUESTIONS

Time of the big light—long dusks, short nights, early mornings. June.

Merle the golden dog, Tinker the sorrel horse, and Ted the Caucasian man gallop across the hay fields in front of their house, between the Teton and Gros Ventre mountains, under the wide Wyoming sky, turning to violet.

The man has worked all day at his desk, writing, making phone calls, balancing a checkbook, and likes the wind in his face, the horse stretched out between his legs so they feel like one creature. The horse has eaten hay, dozed, attacked the horses beneath him in the corral's pecking order, ran from those above him. He's glad to be out, on the move, running where he wants to, the man's hand on his neck, his voice in his ear, "Your go." The dog has visited the other members of his dog community, played chase-me-and-I'll-chase-you-until-we're-so-tired-we'll-all-sleep-in-a-heap, barked at ravens, slept by the man's desk, and is now overjoyed to be with his best buddy, doing what he was made to do: run.

After a mile, the horse slows down exactly as he broke into a gallop: on his own accord. The man dismounts, takes off the horse's headstall and bridle, and lets him graze. Out of sight from the road, buried in sky and swamped by grass, the man lies down, hands behind his head, the dog leaning against his side, and takes a nap.

When he wakes, the sun has long since set behind the Tetons but the valley is lit by the reflected glow of the sky. The man has woken with the sense of being watched, and sure enough, just thirty yards off, a coyote sits, gazing at the horse, the man, and the dog.

The man and the coyote make eye contact and hold it for a few seconds before the coyote walks a little closer, not in a straight line, but in an arc, first away then closer. Twenty yards.

At that moment, Merle, the sleeping dog, wakes and sees the coyote. Before the man's hand can dart to the dog's neck, the dog hurtles toward his wild cousin. Standing, the man sees the two disappear in the tall grass. He calls the horse, bridles him, mounts, and rides in the direction of the two canids.

Within two hundred yards, he sees his dog returning, followed now by two coyotes, only ten yards behind. The three dogs seem easy with each other and in a moment prove it. Merle turns and lopes after the coyotes, who without fear turn and let him chase them for about fifty yards. They then turn and begin to chase Merle, who sets off with a little hop and a shake of his head, both of which seem to say, "Ha ha, this is fun." He lets the coyotes chase him for a hundred or so yards before exchanging roles and becoming the chaser. The coyotes saunter, exhibiting the same sort of golly-this-is-fun lope.

The horse and man break into a canter, catch the dog, and ride alongside him. Suddenly, the two coyotes turn and come at the threesome. The man turns the horse and lets the coyotes chase them for a while, then the horse, man, and dog trot after them. The two groups, chasers and chased, make big circles under the darkening sky. Then the coyotes drift farther and farther northwest, and finally the horse, man, and dog turn slowly and trot toward home.

Unable to transmit with complete accuracy how the horse and dog felt about this evening, I shall speak only for myself. A person need have only a few of these interspecies experiences to know that the creatures of the world are far more complex than most of us imagine. In fact, if you spend enough time outside watching animals, you have to admit that they behave much as we do; and not only do they behave as we do, but they have emotional lives quite similar to our own.

We (both human and nonhuman animals) like to play, we get scared, we love our mates and offspring (sometimes only temporarily), we can be altruistic and compassionate, make practical jokes, enjoy beautiful views, appreciate thoughtfulness in others, revenge wrongdoing, feel shame, be mean, ornery, and even psychopathic, and prefer not to die. Which is the whole point of Jeffrey Masson and Susan McCarthy's book, *When Elephants Weep: The Emotional Lives of Animals.* In short, say the two authors, human and nonhuman animals, particularly mammals, are quite alike.

Sympathetic observers of nature, as well as those who keep pets, have known this for thousands of years. Scientists, on the other hand, have been very reluctant to grant animals the emotional makeup of humans. This has lead to all sorts of horrible ends: René Descartes, the supreme rationalist, conceiving of animals as machines; vivisectionists nailing live dogs to boards by their four paws and cutting them open to examine the circulation of their blood; modern Cartesians dropping irritants into rabbits' eyes so that we can have safe cosmetics; and the domestic meat industry piling chickens and pigs into giant growing factories that resemble nothing so much as concentration camps.

To refute this sort of thinking, Masson and McCarthy fill their book with examples of how animals behave as we do: An elephant helps a young rhino stuck in the mud; a herd of zebras, having already escaped a pack of wild dogs, return to rescue three of their members; an irascible parrot, treated well, becomes friendly. These and hundreds of other anecdotes culled from the literature of field biologists present a compelling case for what Charles Darwin noted: The animal kingdom is united by similar behavior and like sentiment. Unlike Darwin, Masson and McCarthy use their evidence to segue into a discussion of animal rights.

Their last chapter reviews the history of the animal-welfare movement. In 1789, Jeremy Bentham, speaking of animals, said, "The question is not, Can they *reason*? nor, Can they *talk*? but, Can they *suffer*?" In the 1970s, Peter Singer wrote *Animal Liberation*, in which he suggests that sentience, the ability to feel pain, demands that we give equal consideration to the interests of all creatures who possess this quality. In the 1980s, Tom Regan wrote *The Case for Animal Rights*, where he argues that society needs to protect the rights of animals who have a "life story," who are "capable of being the subject of a life."

Masson and McCarthy close this brief account and their call for more compassionate behavior toward animals with one of the Western world's most heartwarming stories of interspecies connection, Androcles and the lion. Androcles, a slave, was brought into the great circus at Rome to be torn to bits by lions. From across the arena, one of the gigantic cats saw him and stopped short in amazement. Approaching the man slowly, he came closer and closer, wagging his tail, and eventually licked the man's feet and hands. The lion and the man then exchanged a joyful greeting. The emperor Caligula, wanting to know why the lion had spared the man, had the slave brought before him. Androcles told him how he had run away from his master and hidden in a cave in the desert. A lion came into the cave, moaning because of a huge splinter in his paw. Spying Androcles, the lion didn't attack. Instead, he lifted his paw in a pleading gesture. Androcles took out the splinter, and in gratitude the lion lay down by his side and they fell asleep together. For three years thereafter they shared the cave, the lion hunting for both of them. Then Androcles was recaptured, sent to Rome, and condemned to death in the circus. Caligula was so moved by Androcles's story that he freed him as well as the lion, allowing them to walk the streets of Rome together.

Whether you believe the details of the story is immaterial. The point is that for three years the lion fed himself and Androcles by hunting other animals—animals who had mates and offspring, felt fear and pain, and more than likely didn't want to die to keep the good lion and the compassionate Androcles going.

Much to Masson and McCarthy's credit, *When Elephants Weep* is not a one-sided book that paints nature as some happy Eden. They discuss warfare among chimpanzees, rape among waterfowl, and revenge in orcas. But they never venture into the really mucky ground that the story of Androcles and the lion raises; namely, if animals and humans are emotionally very similar, and animals can eat each other, is it wrong for humans also to eat animals?

To deflect this question, as many animal welfarists do, with the argument that humans have a conscience and guilt and therefore should treat animals with a hands-off compassion, nullifies the original proposition, which is that animals and humans are alike and so need to be treated similarly. It pulls humans out of nature to defend an ethical stance—in this case animal welfare—and separates humans from nature as surely as the vivisectionists do. Since Masson and McCarthy never address this question—if animals kill for food, why can't humans do likewise?—I'll offer what I think their carefully thought-out answer might be. A dolphin or an orca doesn't have a choice: It must eat fish or sea lions or it will die. Humans, on the other hand, are omnivores. They can eat fish or sea lions or goose-liver paté, but they can also survive quite nicely on tofu.

For most animal welfarists, this makes the question of whether humans can ethically eat animals or use them for utilitarian ends an open-and-shut case. Because we have choice in our diets, we should not kill animals for food. Vegetarianism, including clothing and household products, therefore becomes the least-harm way to live.

And it very well may be. My purpose is not to defend the vegan way of life or to trounce it but to open its modus operandi for deeper inspection. In the process, I hope that we might understand our place in nature with more clarity.

Foremost when thinking about vegetarianism, we must acknowledge the animal lives lost as agribusiness churns out our supermarket vegetables. Rodents, snakes, and birds are poisoned, displaced, and gobbled up by combines as rye, oats, wheat, and soybeans are grown and harvested. Large mammals such as wolves, bears, caribou, and moose are also displaced from the oil fields that fuel farm machinery. Marine life and waterfowl are then killed in oil spills as petroleum products are transported.

These deaths, many animal welfarists will point out, are not perpetrated consciously by the vegan consumer. They are externalities—lamentable and demanding to be eliminated. Yet even as we improve agricultural technologies and slowly turn from fossil fuels, millions of people still need to be fed, and wasted animal lives happen to be one of the costs of modern agriculture. To avoid these costs, we, consumers, can try to buy only organic food, locally grown, or grow it ourselves. This is a conscientious alternative to the supermarket, but it too has costs that must be tallied. I will use a personal example.

When I turn over my garden with a pitchfork or hoe, I frequently impale earthworms, which for many people do not have a "life story" in the way animal-rights philosophers understand that term. In fact, in *Animal Liberation,* Peter Singer places sentience someplace around the level of a mollusk and probably wouldn't grant it to an earthworm. I'm sure Singer wouldn't consciously kill earthworms, but he doesn't give them the same standing as mammals or birds. Yet when I see earthworms writhing on the end of my pitchfork, their reaction does not seem to me to be mere neural response. To speak of an earthworm's writhing in such language reminds me of Cartesian vivisectionists perceiving dogs as "clockworks," so that when they were cut open and howled in agony their cries were understood to be merely the "screech of their inner springs."

If elephants can weep, and chimpanzees laugh, and orioles feel pride at their songs, and dogs howl when they're lacerated, do not earthworms feel pain when stuck with a pitchfork? Do they not have an "earthworm life story," obscure and hidden as it may be to us and the rest of the animal kingdom? And isn't their loss of those stories a cost to weigh against the growing of my organic potatoes? For me, the logic of leaving nature without boundaries of sentience—of investing everyone with the recognition of pain—seems inescapable. Indeed, we are just coming around as a culture, grudgingly and with discomfort, to acknowledging a truth known by cultures that lived closer to the land: Everything is invested with feeling.

Not only do animals not like to die to become another animal's food, but one might make the case, as gathering-hunting cultures have, that trees don't like to be cut for firewood, and when they are they need to be propitiated. Last year, when I moved the stones at the site of my new house to make room for the foundation, I did it with some uneasiness, placing them in new locations with small apologies, hearing John Muir speak words that I had once read but was now feeling: "Why may not even a mineral arrangement of matter be endowed with sensation of a kind that we in our blind exclusive perfection can have no manner of communication with?"

So then, if everyone has feelings—animals, plants, stones— what do we do? How do we move through the world without leaving a wake of suffering? There seem to be three choices, none of which actually alleviates suffering. Rather, each life plan chooses to deal with the pain of other beings in a different way.

The first life plan ignores the pain of others by ignoring all the evidence pointing to the fact that animals feel as we do. It splits humans and nature, putting us in the dominant role. Nature is for our use, it does not feel what we feel, and so we can do just about anything we care to it so long as we're good managers and get a sustained yield.

The second life plan joins humans and nature but draws a distinct line of sentience through it: higher animals have the ability to suffer, lower animals and plants do not, which leaves them open to be used for human food and shelter. Those who choose this life plan can often ignore the real flesh-and-blood animals who die as a result of agricultural practices because those deaths are over the horizon and caused by someone else.

The third life plan joins humans with all of nature, every last bit of it, from the stellar flakes of a geode to the stellar orbs in the heaven, from amoebas to aardvarks. Those who are committed to this sort of joining often experience a profound uneasiness over the question of who dies so others may live.

Another personal example may illustrate this choice. To build my house, I cut standing dead lodgepole pine trees, removing the future homes of sapsuckers and black bears. I could have built a straw-bale home, which in some building circles is considered a more conscientious and ecologically sound structure, but I would have then participated in the slaughter of small-animal populations as the hay was cut with machinery. If I were really conscientious and cut all the hay by hand, I still would have exposed the mice and voles to the sky, causing more of them to be eaten by red-tailed hawks than if the hay had remained uncut. Would I then be culpable for their deaths? I believe I would. Just as I when I drive my car and hit butterflies or bluebirds or Uinta ground squirrels or, every once in a while, a deer, I am responsible for their deaths. There is hardly a motorist on the continent who hasn't participated in this slaughter. A truly caring person would not drive an automobile at all.

The inescapable fact is that in one shape, form, or guise, virtually all of us (mammals, birds, fish, insects, and so on) kill other beings for food, for shelter, or to get from one place to another. We all kill other beings who have—some more, some less—emotions like ours and life stories ranging from one-liners to novels.

How we do this killing, how we permit others to do it for us, where we draw our lines between kingdoms and species, and what kinds of grace we say for the lives that keep us going define how we live out these hardest questions: Why did life evolve based on the death of others? Why is corporeal existence so ephemeral? Why do some of us depart our earthly skins sooner than others, leaving those who cared and loved for us in tears, or in whatever state expresses grief in those beings who don't have lachrymal glands.

If you want to stay in the game—meaning that you decide not to commit suicide and exempt yourself from all future killing—there isn't a single good strategy that lets you live without inflicting some harm. Neither carnivorism, omnivorism, or vegetarianism are adequate solutions, nor is being an organic farmer, a careful livestock grower, or an aboriginal hunter-gatherer. Some life plans, of course, are more clear-sighted than others. Whichever we choose, we can try to take gently those lives that support us, offering thanks for their gifts, and rejoicing often that we are given another day.

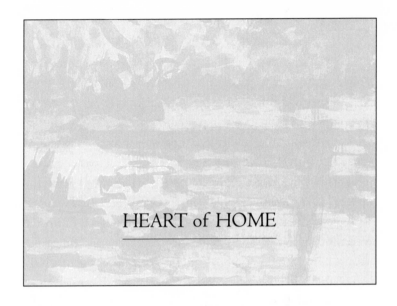

HEART of HOME

September 3

So you really can't count on anything except change, losing and refinding the people you love, though today I can only see the loss. I walk uphill, through the red rock and from spruce grove to aspen forest along the rim of a plateau. The wind blows warmly and the aspen are still green from the wet spring and summer. The Gros Ventre mountains, their craggy summits dusted with snow, retreat toward the east and join the glaciers of the Wind Rivers. Heading toward the sky, I still count on my legs, but even they feel tired.

It rained through the spring and into the summer, rain mixed with snow, often snow alone, the wettest year ever recorded in northwestern Wyoming. The first hatch of grouse was killed, as well as most of the second, so these groves, usually so reliable for producing birds, seem swept clean of life, which is about how I feel as well.

On the other side of the plateau, I descend a long nave of

aspen, where I made my only double on grouse: one bird flushed straight down this trail; another flared left. Marking the first's fall, I turned and dropped the second as it crossed an opening in the canopy. Amazing. Never repeated.

He enjoyed hearing about that kind of wing shooting and of course eating the birds themselves, holding half a roasted grouse in his hands, the grease on his mouth catching the glow of the fire. On his last healthy visit, we ate those two birds and watched elk bugle in the frosty mornings and drove through Yellowstone to the hot springs, walking around the cauldrons and fumaroles because he still could walk. Back in the cabin, after the first blizzard of the year, he stood by the woodstove, hands outstretched, cheeks red, while huffing a litany of curses in Greek about the bitter cold and the slowness of the kindling. The words, which would have been crude if translated, were sweet as a poem. Not only were they foreign and musical, but they were also the language of his immigrant parents, my grandparents, and full of memories. I made him coffee, and, warmed, he looked at the blueprints for the new house. When I pointed out the guest rooms that I was adding for him and Mom and mentioned how happy I'd be when they'd stay for a couple of months, watching the seasons change, the elk migrate, he said, "God willing, God willing." Always it was "God willing."

I guess this time he wasn't. Or maybe I just wasn't quick enough in getting the house done.

The sun arcs over the mountains, falling away south toward the solstice, and I can still feel my hand on his casket as we lowered it into the ground, the sunlight glaring on the mahogany lid just where his face lay underneath, the edge of the grave making a line of moving shadow, a line of light and darkness rising toward his head. Then the line of shadow took him and he was gone: my dad, or the part of him I could hold in my arms and who had held me, gone . . . my hand hanging in the air as flowers sailed past me and down into his grave like the fall of shooting stars.

I walk on through the trees, the side-by-side shotgun over my shoulder, a preference descended from the first double-barreled gun he gave me when I was twelve years old. The first fishing rod he gave me at four, the two of us walking hand in hand down to the lake. A .22 rifle at ten, all the surf and blue-water rods, the cameras, and that lovely Mont Blanc fountain pen, his voice so pleased as he handed it to me, "You are a writer. You should have one good pen."

These gifts were his way of sharing in activities that he, a city boy, didn't totally enjoy or never wanted to repeat. He told me once of hunting, "I did enough of that in the war." His gifts were also a letting go, an allowing me to be whomever I dreamed. For a man who had lost his boyhood and education to early work, leaving high school to help support his mother, sisters, and a slipshod and invalid father, allowing his children to dream was his way of enjoying the dreams he himself had missed. And although I appreciated the equipment, those gifts were nothing compared to his love itself. Along with my mother, he was a safety net, uncritical as bedrock and just as permanent. As I left on a year-and-a-half-long journey to the other side of the world, he gave me one of his great bear hugs and said, "Be careful. I love you. I will miss you. If you need anything, *Etho imaste.*" The last again said in Greek, the language in which he frequently thought and breathed: "*Here* we are, always." He was a radio beam, sending his love, our connection, through the stratosphere, finding me no matter where I was.

Cumulus clouds, stately as clippers, float over the canopy of aspen, and I stand, mute and transfixed by them, wondering where he is flying now and trying to see him as he was—sometimes heavy and with a double chin, sometimes lean from all the running, his weight constantly flip-flopping, his grin an eternal flame, fueled by the presence of his family. How do I now say, "This was the color of the sky as I walked today, the grouse are gone because of the early rains, and Merle, your favorite golden dog, is strong and fine, running ahead of me; the horses are well, and I miss you, miss you." Where do I send these thoughts? There are no more letters to write. There is no more phone to his ear, only my heart direct to his on the September wind.

September 24

The air fills with elk bugles, and Scott and I head to the park with our binoculars, some beer, and some elk jerky. We walk the abandoned road at sunset, squeals and grunts from the rutting bull elk floating from the trees on our right. On our left, two large bulls appear suddenly in a sprawling meadow and chase a female across it and into the forest. Above them loom the gray spires of the Tetons, dusted with new snow.

We wait, and as the dusk deepens elk seep out of the trees. Three mature bulls—six points on each side of their antlers—as well as an unusual seven-point elk come into the meadow. They are followed by a not-often-seen eight-pointer, who looks too large to be of this age. Ivory tines gleaming, he seems out of the Pleistocene.

One of the six-pointers walks toward us, stopping about a hundred yards off. He coughs belligerently in our direction, then bugles at us. He has to turn quickly, for the seven-pointer has blind-sided him and chases him toward the trees. The eight-point elk trots after them. At the edge of the forest, the seven-pointer stops, wheels, and charges the larger bull. Their antlers rattle like the clang of ancient swords. Then it's so dark that the two elk appear as no more than dark shapes on the grassy meadow, their breaths spouting like silver clouds as they spar and separate and bugle.

I turn to Scott, seeing only the glimmer of his copper-colored hair. He's the director of finance for the Teton Science School and is big, steady, precise, and strong. Also quiet. It is good to see him get excited. Grinning enormously, he says, "By Jesus."

October 1

Merle and I ride through the old burn on the south side of Shadow Mountain. He lopes in front; I pedal behind him, the mountain bike in low-low gear. Charred and skeletal, the pines line the Forest Service road. By sight, I mark the straightest with boles about a foot in diameter. They're the easiest to fell and split for firewood. Tomorrow we'll come back with the truck and cut.

I'm also looking for grouse but halfheartedly. They seem to be nowhere and, to be truthful, I haven't been in the mood for hunting. At the top of the hill, I scout a good turnaround for the pickup, then coast back through the long meadows, standing on the pedals, riding the bumps, the air warm, the Tetons like the jagged back of an ancient dinosaur protecting the western side of the valley.

In a wide meadow, the grass waist-high and blowing, the bike rolls to a stop. I straddle the top bar and watch the mountains, the sky, and the drift of the puffy clouds, feeling the seat poke me from behind like the unexpected shove of a friend. He was the first person I knew to own a ten-speed bike, a gold one with dropped handlebars wrapped in white tape. On Saturdays, he took us—son, cousins, friends—like some cycling Pied Piper, down the roads along the bays, deep into the cool maple forests, along the stone walls, wearing a white T-shirt and trouser clips to hold his baggy long pants out of the chain. It was the highlight of the day when he let each of us ride "the big bike," our feet barely touching the pedals.

And on Sundays, he took us clamming, our bushel baskets floating in inner tubes, the tubes tied to our waists with long cords, so we could rake and dig, waist deep in water, without worrying about the baskets floating away. Returning to the house, we opened dozens of clams—cherrystones, just the size of a tennis ball and his favorite. Sitting at the long picnic table under the acacia trees, we ate them, dozen after dozen with pasta and lemonade—beer when we were older—eating through the dusk and lighting citronella candles against the mosquitoes, the citronella mixing with the smell of horseradish and lemon and the clean sea smell of the clams.

He too was clean-smelling as a clam, insisting on showering before sitting down to dinner. Except when he first came down the street after work and I ran toward him under the long alley of maple trees, one of their seedpods stuck to my nose like a green rhino's horn. Into his arms I jumped, and he whirled me round and round, my feet flying, my nose pressed against his chest and warm sweaty smell.

Where are you now, Pop?

He seems right there in the precipices of the Grand Teton, smiling along the bottom edges of purple clouds, talking in the grass. I wrap my arms around myself as if he were right here in my arms and feel the mountains wrap themselves around me just as he, my ever-constant, hugged me. Merle puts both paws on my thigh and looks at me. Putting an arm around his neck, I rough his cheek, then pick some grass and throw it toward the sky, toward the four directions, as I did at his grave.

Fly on, Pop, fly on.

Mounting the seat, I pedal through the old burn, feeling my childhood between my legs.

October 8

In town, sixteen miles down valley and 6,200 feet high, it's raining. At the house, five hundred feet higher, we have wet snow. A thousand feet higher up the mountain, new powder. Benj, my old riding and kayaking partner, sometime hunting buddy, has come up from Utah, cheery with his new job at the university and the ten pounds he has shed. We talk into the night and then climb quickly by starlight, hearing cow elk bark at us from a stand of lodgepoles. Even though we wait silently in the new snow, they drift away. Shooting light still an hour off, we gain the ridge, hike toward Three Basin Saddle, and spook a spike bull, whom Benj sees for a second. Tracking him, we find the spoor of three more elk, but they are in high gear and we never catch them. I think of the wolves I've watched hunting in Yellowstone this spring—they test so many animals before finding one who mistakes a sound, strays from its herd, falters, and becomes meat, and so do we.

The sun rises and Benj and I sit next to each other on the crest of the pass, big lodgepoles at our backs, the three basins falling away before us. The cirques above them emerge from fuming clouds, and far below us the creeks appear as slate-gray lines through the forest. Nothing moves except a raven, and there's no sound except its caw and the pulse of my heart in my ears. Sinking into the quiet, I stare at the elk tracks fifty yards below us. They are like marks on a test about our ability to walk with stealth, about our moving with the speed of dawn, and we failed. Or, with a more positive spin, we are regaining fluency. Each autumn, the first stalks are like coming back to a well-known foreign land from which we've been absent. We lose our summer tourist clothes, the easy relationship between hiker and animals, and put on the clothes of predator and prey.

By noon, we're home, drinking strong coffee and eating home fries from my garden potatoes. The phone rings. It's Dorothy Bishop, calling for her husband, Norm, who's up on a ridge above the Circle JP, skinning out a moose he killed this morning. Any chance I could bring up my horses and pack it out? She'll leave a trail of surveyor tape.

We trailer the horses to the roadhead, follow her orange markers, and find Dorothy and Norm in a foot of snow, surrounded by moose quarters. Nearing retirement with the Park Service, Norm is as thin as a cross-country ski and in athletic shape. Nevertheless, he straightens up with a groan, holds the small of his back, and says, "I am tired." Benj and I help them finish boning out the rib cage, then we load the two packhorses with the quarters, hide, and the Bishops' gear, so they get a free walk down. Riding Whisk, my sorrel horse, I lead the pack string through the pines, the mulched smell of wet ground and working horses pungent, the aspens sifting the light. Below us, I can see the roofs of the ranch, where the Bishops began their hunt, and where Scott lives with his wife, April, a teacher at the Teton Science School, and their fourteen-month-old daughter, Tessa.

We unload the horses in the last light. As the frosty stars appear, we sit before the stone fireplace, the fir trees around the house bringing the northern forest right up to the windows. In an old gesture, we hold hands, say a grace for the gathering of these friends, for our continued health, and for the moose who was walking this morning and who feeds us now.

October 18

Hiking along the Salt River in the dark, in the lashing rain, I listen to Dusty rave on about unemployed fishing guides—the young punks of the valley who steal his duck-hunting spots, shoot his waterfowl, and live off birds and their girlfriends' paychecks all fall.

Carrying my bucket and my side-by-side shotgun, I listen. Dusty looks like a cross between Rasputin and Paul Bunyan and comes from Louisiana. In a land of elk hunters, deer hunters, and sheep hunters, he hunts ducks, and still hunts ducks though he has lived in Wyoming for years. He has a stash of duck-hunting spots on the local rivers and can't believe that other people are now discovering them. I tell him Wyoming's getting crowded, and he grunts.

He has set up the decoys the night before, so all we have to do is sit on our buckets in the willows, the rain pouring down, the mountains looming above us in the clouds. Payhas, Dusty's young chocolate Lab, trembles with anticipation.

The slough we overlook is no more than forty yards across. The wind comes downriver from the left, and the birds— wigeon, gadwall, and mallards—fly upriver from the right in pairs, sixes, tens. Cupping their wings, they begin to land in our decoys. I shoot five birds with six shots, Dusty four birds with five shots, and because the birds are close when we shoot, they drop like stones at the sound of the guns, plopping dead into the water or bouncing on the far bank.

Payhas brings me one of the largest drake mallards I have ever killed, and I sit with the lovely fat bird in my hand as the rain tapers off. His head is iridescent green, his feet an astounding orange. Above us, the clouds foam like a pewter sea broken with ragged holes. Through them, shafts of light pour, illuminating distant hillsides where stands of aspen and pods of willow shine like tarnished gold.

I have not shot one grouse, my favorite bird, this fall, and the elk haven't migrated yet because of good grass above tree line and lack of snow. But duck numbers are up, and here are five birds at my feet and a morning out of my teenage years, when waterfowl blackened the skies.

October 28

First big party at the new house. Friends up from Colorado, but the snow is crunchy as popcorn. First thing in the morning, we spook about fifteen elk, whom we can hear moving through the timber. Then, we hike along the ridges for miles, stopping, glassing, and listening but not seeing or hearing any more animals. At home, the clear day descends into a lucid dusk. Jupiter and the crescent moon hover together over the Tetons like lovers.

Tired from the long day, everyone turns in early. But I can't sleep and I sit with a glass of port, looking out the big window at the Milky Way and at the red glass candleholder, resting on the sill, that I brought back from Dad's funeral. Mom wanted me to leave the candle lit in their church, at the foot of altar, under the icons and the eyes of Jesus. But I wanted it here, under the eyes of the sky, and she understood right away. I lit it on the Wednesday afternoon that I returned, working the next three days at the office, and watching the candle at night, the flame moving downward inside the red glass. Three and a half days later, on Sunday morning just as I was waking, I heard the candle fizzle out. Coming downstairs, I saw a wisp of smoke rising into the air. At that precise moment, the sun rose over the Gros Ventre mountains— a shaft of light came through the kitchen window and struck the candle exactly where it smoked. I stood transfixed . . . then did my grouse walk, looking for a trace of his smoke in the sky.

I have another glass of port—the wine of the church, of old British sea captains, of *hacendados*, of my college in London, and now this house, with its wine cellar and root cellar. Dad preferred whiskey and big heavy cars with names like DeSoto and Oldsmobile and, back when men wore dress hats, a fedora pulled low over his eyes. Wine cellars, small cars with four-wheel drive named Subaru, ski hats and snowpacks, colleges in London—he could understand them for his son and his daughter, Rene, with their degrees and love of *The New York Times Book Review*. He himself read the New York *Daily News*.

Did we really spend a lifetime tugging at each other? He wanting me to be more diligent and dapper. I wanting him to be outdoorsy and esthetic. We gave each other the occasional treats—I wore a three-piece suit and once in a while shaved off my beard. He came camping and read everything I wrote, my most constant fan. And though I could tell him all about patience in the outdoors, waiting through an entire night for one fish, I failed miserably in being patient with women, which he knew quite clearly and told me often to correct. But I didn't listen to him for a long, long time. And though he was kind to a fault, and loving to the point of self-denial when it came to providing for his family, he became ever more obnoxious with drink, which I told him, which we all told him many times, and he didn't listen, at least not for a long, long time. Until that Christmas, twenty I think I was, when I grabbed him by the shirtfront, pushed him against the wall in the hallway, and crying with anger, frustration, and shame—my father, the drunk—landed the punch right by the side of his head, dishing in the plaster with my rage instead of his face.

Horrified, I ran out of the house and walked for miles. In the morning I found a letter: his apology and promise. The way he had given up smoking, throwing his cigarette into the trash and never looking back, he pretty much gave up hard drinking, having the occasional beer or glass of wine with dinner. Patience with love, unfortunately, it took me longer to find. But then, he was older than I when we started each other's educations.

November 3

Glade Creek. The long walk down to the park boundary along the Snake River. One lone elk track and no new snow. The elk haven't migrated yet.

November 4

First rough-legged hawk. Jupiter, Mars, and Venus set in a line on the west horizon. Tired and to bed early.

November 5

Sheep Creek in a whiteout and lashing, horizontal snow. Above a rocky basin, in a small meadow, I find dozens of elk prints. The herd has scuffed off the snow down to the grass. But it's nearly dark when I find the tracks, which descend into tangled, north-facing forest. As I drive home, snow swirls in the headlights. I creep along the unplowed road and into storms past. When the house burned down from the chimney fire and I was left temporarily homeless, I did actually go back to my first home, to see Mom and Dad and Rene and to be at Pete and Sharon's wedding. Then Dad and I drove back to the Rockies through three days of blizzards. Three January days in the car, talking about his childhood, climbing, the war, women, my girlfriends, his wife, and his and Mom's argumentative relationship. They had bickered nearly the entire time I had been home. He looked shocked when I mentioned it.

"We don't mean anything by that," he said.

"Could have fooled me."

"We always say good night to each other and 'I love you.' "

"If I were you, I might have divorced her years ago." Once I had said the very same thing to my mother about him.

My father now looked truly disturbed, as if he couldn't believe I was under such a gross misapprehension. He held out his palm, cupped upward gently, the way he always offered a truism. Using virtually the same words my mother had once used about him, he said, "But she has a heart of gold."

By the time I get home, the world is totally white, winter is here, and I'm hoping the elk will now be on the move.

November 10

Winter doesn't come. It continues to rain and sleet. Postholing, Scott and I hike up Breadloaf Mountain, through the old burn, and look down to the Snake, plates of ice in the shallows leading to Jackson Lake, which is slate gray and foreboding. We note two elk tracks in two hours. Nothing moves except the wind.

November 22

Rain and more rain. Rain for days. Ice and crust. Abominable walking. Still, Scott has seen elk at the big bend of Ditch Creek, but he didn't take a shot—the animals were spooked and running, trees in the way. We drive my truck up the creek road, the mud and slush over the hubs, and climb two different spurs in the late afternoon, the snow crunching horribly. Lots of tracks but no live elk.

The sun sets in a streak of whitish-yellow over Jackson Peak, giving the soggy landscape a forlorn air.

November 24

Day after Thanksgiving. Big dinner at the house—elk and a Canada goose from last year. Scott, April, Tessa, some of the old Ditch Creek crew, Merle, and I take a hike, eat for hours, then at five in the morning Scott and I head up toward Mount Leidy on snowshoes. Not a track except those of moose, weasel, and squirrel. Only two weeks left in elk season.

Back at the ranch, Scott makes us tea. I sit by the window, by the fire, with Tessa. The skylight glints on her copper-colored hair, just like Scott's. We read an animal book that squeaks out the animal's voice when you press one of its pictures.

"Elephant." She presses it. A trumpet.

"Dog." She presses it. Bowwow. She immediately points to Merle, sleeping on the rug before us. "Moo-moo," she says, using her name for him.

I point to me.

"Teee-ed," she says, giving me a big proud smile and putting her hand on my chest.

The long days hiking through the snow fall away. Forgetful editors, unreliable subcontractors, swamped auto mechanics—everyone to whom I listened on my answering machine when I called it from the ranch—disappear.

Pop had it right. "If you have love in your life, it can make up for a great many things you lack. If you don't have it, no matter what else there is, it's not enough."

November 27

The interminable rain finally turns to snow, dropping a couple of inches on the valley floor. Scott and I leave at four-thirty in the morning and are in the parks above the Buffalo River at first light. Plenty of moose tracks but not an elk track to be seen. Underneath the new snow is a rain crust that breaks at every step. We posthole up to our knees and crotches. Dumb—leaving the snowshoes in the car. We split up. I climb to the foot of Mount Randolph and find the high country deep in winter. Glassing, listening, Merle and I see nothing. On the way back, I find five elk tracks on the first bench, not a hundred yards from where Scott and I separated. But they're from the middle of the night.

November 30

Back in the Buffalo, one of the three elk areas remaining open. On snowshoes, trying to stay off the crust, Scott and I hunt above Lava Creek, crossing many, many tracks from the day before. Scott sees a six-point bull at thirty yards, but only cows are legal now. I watch five cows descend a slope across the valley from me, disappear into a stand of trees, and never reappear.

On the way out, we meet Greg, who owns one of the local sporting-goods stores in town and who is a fine kayaker and climber. He mentions that he's been watching elk on Davis Hill, across Lava Creek, but because of the steep climb down and back up and how difficult it will be to bring an elk out of that country, too steep even for horses, he hasn't gone over by himself. He suggests that the three of us team up and go over tomorrow morning, which we decide to do.

Back at the office, I write. I've never seen a November so gray and dull as this one. It seems to be first light the entire day, the clouds hanging so low that you might have thought there wasn't a mountain within miles. Snow falls. Gray Cat lies on the desk, Merle at my feet. I look at Dad's photo in the Wind Rivers. He kneels by a creek in his long johns, his face just splashed with morning water, his grin radiating from his tan.

The evening before, I had sat in the door of the tent, watching the stars. Napping, he woke and sat next to me, just listening to the awesome silence of the mountains. After a while, he said, "You sure do love this place."

"It's home."

"It's so quiet." He smiled. "It drives me crazy."

I look at him and Mom, arm in arm, strong and healthy, on the Mexican schooner. He loved to say, "She saved my life."

"What do you mean?"

We were eating buffalo burgers up in Yellowstone, outside in the dusk, father and son on one of their long drives.

"Oh, I was a wild guy. I would have been a bum without her, you know."

On my face, a look of disbelief.

"Truth. She made me into a good person."

I uncover the last photo: I by his side in his wheelchair; the ever-present oxygen bottle and nose tube; still the grin but faded and his arm around my waist like a vise. Of me and my sister he always said, "You are my life."

I shuffle the photos. Three are missing: Rene and me at the dinner table, shoulder to shoulder, heads leaning together, smiling for him; Merle and me on a huge boulder on the Yellowstone

River, high summer, the grass like Eden; and the new log house, the Gros Ventres rising behind it like a mythic land of fir and aspen and snow. Now the three photos are in his breast pocket along with the sage, clover, and purple aster, picked from in front of the house. Sealed in with him, they send him along. I stare into the clouds and still feel his arm around my waist—that eternal vise.

December 1

It takes us an hour and fifteen minutes by headlamp to descend through the north-facing deadfall to Lava Creek. We follow elk tracks down and then up the opposite hillside. We leave Scott off first, on a knoll above a steep basin, and I follow Greg to the next valley. Greg goes on to the last.

After putting on my warm clothing, I drink a mug of tea. Warm in my gut, I look down the steep slopes to Lava Creek. Nothing moves, not even a raven. Nothing sounds, not even the patter of pinecone bracts dropped on the snow by a squirrel.

The silence makes the shot, booming above me a little after first light, sound so startling, final, and sure. About a half hour later, Scott walks up, saying that he doesn't have good feelings about this spot. He's going to wait a bit longer then walk back across the creek and hunt the north-facing trees opposite us.

I wait a little longer, hoping for an elk who I know won't come. Resigned, I climb up the ridge, seeing what I expected: Greg with his sleeves rolled up, his arms bloody, and a cow elk lying gutted in the snow. Tomorrow will be another early morning for me.

A small herd crossed the ridge below him, he tells me, several bulls, a few cows and calves. The lead bull had actually put his nose into Greg's boot prints, smelled them, and looked up the ridge, where he spotted Greg crouched behind a deadfall. As the herd stared at him, Greg shot expertly between the bull's antlers, hitting a more distant cow in the neck.

He uncoils his rope, says graciously, "Keep hunting, I can get her down," and begins the long drag to the creek. I head up the steep ridge, kicking steps in the deepening snow, enjoying the fresh pine smell, the sky half clearing with great patches of blue. It's eight o'clock. I know I won't see any animals, but I like the climb and the view is more than worth the effort: the Tetons sprawl across the western horizon, visible for the first time in days.

Crossing several elk runs, four feet wide and trampled into mud, I continue toward the summit. Then the snow becomes deeper, and I plod on, hunting into the wind.

Just as I approach the top, I smell elk musk on the breeze. Surprised, I look left and down into the basin where a dozen elk run through the snow. At that instant, a high-pitched shot comes from the ridge that I just climbed. There stands a hunter in a white anorak and orange hat, about three hundred yards off, shooting at the running herd below me. His rifle sounds like a cap gun.

Astonished and unnerved, I hesitate a moment, then decide. It's two days from the end of elk season and nothing this fall, beginning with Dad's death, has happened as I wished. I choose a large cow, follow her in the sight, saying my apologies, but still not liking how fast things are happening or that there is another hunter popping up from nowhere and shooting in my direction.

My rifle cracks, the elk lurches but doesn't go down. Now she heads directly away from me, her herd mates to each side of her. I hate this shot—at an elk's back who is scared and running away